SAVING SEEDS

The Complete Guide To Starting, Growing And Storing Vegetables, Fruits, Herbs And Flowers Seeds

NATHAN RIVERA

The statistics in this paper are primarily for educational purposes and are all-inclusive. The data are entered without a contract or any confirmation of assurance.

The trademarks used are without consent and the trademark distribution is without the consent or support of the trademark owner. Both trademarks in the book are solely for the purpose of illustrating and are clearly managed and not associated by the founders.

TABLE OF CONTENTS

ABOUT THE BOOK 1

INTRODUCTION 7

THE COMPLETE GUIDE TO GROWING AND STORING
VEGETABLES, FRUITS, HERBS AND FLOWERS SEEDS 15

KEEPING THE GARDEN FREE FROM RABBITS 22

HOW TO GROW VEGETABLES IN WINTER 30

AQUAPONICS-HOW TO GROW VEGETABLES QUICKLY 35

HOW TO GROW VEGETABLES IN CONTAINERS 41

COMMON VEGETABLE GARDENING PROBLEMS..................... 50

IMPORTANT TOOLS THAT ARE USEFUL FOR VEGETABLE
GARDENING.. 61

HOW TO PLANT A FLOWER GARDEN FOR BEAUTY AND
FUNCTION.. 65

HOW TO GET BEAUTIFUL FLOWERS WITHOUT DAMAGING
YOUR BUDGET 68

PROBLEMS GROWING FLOWERS....................................... 71

HOW TO MANAGE GROWING TOMATOES 82

HOW TO GROW LETTUCE 86

HOW TO GROW BROCCOLI SPROUTS.................................. 92

HOW TO GROW APPLE TREES FROM A SEED 97

HOW TO GROW ARTICHOKES... 103

HOW TO GROW ASPARAGUS 111

HOW TO GROW ASPARAGUS 114

HOW TO GROW GRAPES 117

PROPAGATION REQUIREMENTS.. 121

HOW TO GROW BLACKBERRIES 124

GROWING, PLANTING AND PROPAGATING GREEN BEANS ... 130

PROBLEMS GROWING HERBS 137

HERBS AND DISEASE 142

PROPAGATION REQUIREMENTS OF POTATOES 145

PROPAGATION REQUIREMENTS OF MAIZE 149

GENERAL CARE AND MAINTENANCE 151

CONCLUSION 155

ABOUT THE BOOK

Saving seeds from your garden plants not only lower planting costs, but it's also a perfect way to witness your garden plants' entire life cycle. This article discusses how seeds can be collected and processed from your flowers and vegetable plants.

The garden starts in January for several gardeners when the first catalog of seeds arrives in the mailbox. While the freezing wind is hurling outside, we retire to a comfortable chair and leaf through the catalog, carefully noting which varieties of lettuce and tomatoes to try and wish we had the room to plant each flower displayed so artfully on its covers.

But have you ever wondered where your grandparents bought the seeds for their gardens before catalogs of seeds and fancy garden centers became available?

They were saving seeds from their gardens for the next year!

Saving seeds from your flowers or vegetables is a great way to understand the plant growth process completely. It's also much less costly than buying seeds every spring, and seeds saved from your plants would be well suited to the peculiarities of growing conditions in your own backyard. Not just that, it's a very easy operation too.

Only save seeds from vigorous, stable plants. Many plant diseases can be harbored in the seed, where they will then be transferred to the next plant generation. So, do not save seeds from a plant that is clearly ill or that has suffered all season. Select seeds from plants with the properties you like, such as height, hardness, early or late maturation, flavor or vigor.

Saving seeds from hybrid plants isn't recommended. Hybrids are the result of the fusion of two genetically distinct parent plants, both of which have been highly inbred to concentrate the desirable properties. Referred to as an F1 hybrid, the first generation is equivalent to parents. But subsequent generations of plants grown from seed saved from an F1 plant appear to return spontaneously to the characteristics of original ancestor inbred plants.

Plants that are not hybrids are considered open-pollinated plants. Many catalogs of seeds will classify which of their seeds is hybrid or open-pollinated. When you decide to save your own seed, continue with open-pollinated seeds at all times. Some of these can also be known as seeds which are heirloom. Such varieties of heirloom have been passed down for decades, often held for several years within a single family before being available to the general public.

Another issue for the seed-saving gardener is cross-pollination. Cross-pollination also results in seeds that have a genetic makeup different from that of the parent plant. Pumpkins, squash and small gourds will cross-pollinate with each other, leading to seeds that grow to produce very picturesque fruit. Sweet corn with field corn or popcorn will cross-pollinate and your 6-inch marigolds will overlap with the 18-inch pompon marigolds of your neighbor. The crossing can only take place within one species, however. Cucumbers do not go well with peas, and pansies do not go with other plant species.

Make sure that two varieties of the same plant are separated by as much space as possible to prevent cross-pollination.

Some plants, including corn, are pollinated by wind, and the pollen can fly great distances. These plants must be hand-pollinated and kept separate from other species. For example, this can be achieved by placing a small paper bag over selected ears before the silk appears, then after the silk appears, it is hand-pollinated with pollen from the same plant or its healthy neighbors.

Seeds should be harvested on a warm, dry day. Some seeds don't become frozen as long as the seed stays intact. Before their seeds are collected, vegetables such as cucumbers, peppers, and tomatoes should be allowed to become some-what overripe. Flower seeds and vegetable seeds such as lettuce should be collected after the seed heads have become dry, but don't wait too long, because many will break, meaning that if they stay on the plant for too long they will be dropped from the seedpod or seed head.

Cucumber, squash, and tomato seeds require a further phase before they are ready to be processed. Next, they have to extract the seeds from the pulp, then dried. From these vegetables scoop the seeds, the pulp and all. Place the whole mess in a water jar, and mix well, then let it settle a little. The pulp rises to the top while the seeds fall downwards. Pour out the pulp carefully, then repeat the process until most of the pulp is drained out. Then strain the seeds out and put them to dry on newspapers.

Seeds should get as dry as possible and then placed into storage. Give all seeds a drying time of at least a week after harvest, just to be sure they are dry. Spread them out in the sun as they dry on a paper plate or newspapers in a warm place.

Keeping the seed dry when in storage is very necessary. Place your dry seeds in tightly packed pots, metal film containers or old bottles of vitamins. Smaller amounts of multiple seed varieties can be stored in separate envelopes inside a jar to save space. A cold, but never freezing garage, closed-off spare room or cold basement can all be good locations for seed storage. Just keep your packed seed jars in the fridge. Temperatures from 32 to 41 degrees Celsius are optimal.

Be sure to mark your jars and envelopes so that when spring returns, you'll know what flower seeds and vegetable seeds you're planting, including the date the seeds were collected. Several seeds will remain viable for many years, but most will grow better if they are immediately planted the following spring.

Seek this year to save some vegetable or flower seeds from your greenhouse and cultivate them next season. This endless cycle will allow you to realize the endless joy of gardening across all the seasons and stages in the life of a plant.

INTRODUCTION

Saving seeds has long been the primary means of moving plants from generation to generation. Seed Saving is not only enjoyable, but it is also a meaningful way of perpetuating heirloom plants and ensuring the genetic diversity of food crops worldwide, which erodes at an unparalleled and accelerating rate. Over the years, seed saving has been successfully used for many crops. Essentially, the varieties we call "heirloom" are here today, because committed gardeners like you and me have saved seed faithfully over the years.

Seeds are saved from annual and biennial plants, in general. Seeds that you save are accustomed to your climate and growing medium from your home production system and are adapted to the pests in your field. Seeds from hybrid varieties produce a variety of offspring, many of which may have characteristics different from the parent. Saving seed is easy; people have done it for thousands of years, sustaining all the wonderful vegetables that we eat today in the process.

Saving seed allows you to grow plants to maturity, and eventually they get bigger and live longer than normal, so leave a little more space around them when planting. Saving and rising seed is a part of evolution year after year. Saving seeds from heritage plants or plants native to your region is a way to preserve the diversity in the environment. Saving garden seeds can be a perfect cost-saving measure at the end of each growing season and a way to replicate the delectable harvest last year.

Plants are pollinated by wind, insects or by what is known as self-pollination in three different ways. Plants of the same species may overlap with each other creating parent plant mixes. As with beans, plants with pods are ready when the pods are brown and dry. Wind-pollinated plants (such as corn and spinach) and insect-pollinated plants (such as squash and cucumbers) produce a next-generation that has similar characteristics of the "parent plant," or they may cross with other varieties to create something completely unique. There has been a major shift in recent decades to buying seed annually from commercial seed suppliers, and to seed hybridized or cloned plants that do not yield seed that remains "true to type " – retaining the characteristics of the parent. To be effective in seed saving, new skills need to be developed to improve growers' ability to ensure desirable properties are retained in their plant. It is the understanding of the minimum number of plants to be grown that will maintain inherent genetic diversity and knowing the cultivar's chosen characteristics so that plants that are not true to breeding are not selected for seed production. Recommended minimum seed survival plant count: 25 cucumbers, squash, melons; 50-100 radishes, brassicas, mustards; 200 sweet corn. Since the plants have been properly separated from different varieties of the same species, seed saved from these plants should grow well.

When randomly matted inside their range, the open-pollinated varieties should grow true to nature. If two spinach varieties bloom near each other, then the resulting seed is likely to be a cross between the two. To prevent cross-pollination, different pepper varieties should be separated by 500 feet. The closer the varieties, the greater the number of seeds crossed. Theoretically, you can aim to separate all varieties for at least half a mile.

Heirloom vegetables are varieties which farmers and gardeners grow, pick, save, name and share. Heirloom plants are now accessible because seeds for domestic use have been saved by people throughout the centuries of subsistence agriculture. Through planting with heirloom seeds, you can really cut down on your gardening costs which will help you to save year after year. You can also save seeds from the heirloom flowers including cleome, foxgloves, hollyhock, nasturtium, sweet pea and zinnia. You are in charge of the varieties of heirloom which do best in your garden. Saving your own seeds will improve your self-sufficiency and save you money. It's known as an heirloom generally. A variety must be open-pollinated.

Since heirloom seeds and the seed saving method still hold hope for helping to feed a hungry world, today it's more beneficial. You can save favorite heirloom seeds in your garden for your own use, breed and improve varieties, trade with others, join seed-saving groups, or grow seed commercially at any scale — there are numerous opportunities.

Once you store the seeds, make sure you have dried them thoroughly. Once thoroughly dried and stored in air-proof containers in the freezer for extended storage or in a cool, dry cellar for next season, the quality home-saved seeds will be maintained. While some vegetable seeds will remain viable in storage for as long as 15 years or more and grains will remain viable even longer under stable environmental conditions, the amount of seed that will germinate will decrease each year in storage. It helps to buy desiccant packets for your storage containers to keep your seeds dry when you've processed the seeds and are ready to pack for the winter. During storage, seeds should contain 3-5 percent moisture. In the case of worldwide catastrophes, war, pandemic outbreaks and other unexpected disasters, storing seeds will safeguard the vegetation of the planet.

If you are a beginner organic gardener, reliable sources of seed will be required to start your seed bank. Even if you don't want to save plants, many people worry about the origins of their seeds and want to steer clear of genetically modified seeds. So, how do you understand that the seeds you buy are safe and good for organic production?

Research Farms: i.e. private research farms dedicated to finding and applying environmentally sound methods, are the first place to look.

Seed Companies: search for seed companies engaged in the marketing of open-pollinated crops. Open pollination occurs when plants are left to reproduce through wind, birds, and bees on their own. But hybrid seeds are not always bad. Hybrids are two or more crop crossbreeds bred for their strengths. For example, a farmer takes a tomato that normally lasts longer against certain diseases in his area, and then he breeds it with a variety that is known to be producing early—if it produces early, the disease will never develop. These two properties combine to make the variety strong and the product can reach the market earlier. Many other farmers may like the variety and would like to purchase some of the crop. Okay, when they know the exact varieties used to produce the plant, they'll have to buy seed from the original breeder.

Selection: three or four companies that suit the bill are picked. Order seeds from each one. It doesn't need to be a big order. Simply order something small, evaluate customer service and seeds. Plant, and examine the results. If you're happy you may have several seed sources. I use Johnny's Selected Plants, Bountiful Crops, and Southern Seed Exchange as the three seed companies. I don't have any association with these businesses, but they provide excellent customer support, ships fast and deliver on their promise.

Market farmers: who are devoted to organic and open-pollinated seeds are another great seed source. Those seeds are specially grown for the market. You will have seeds for your garden next season if you buy their seed-bearing produce.

Avid Gardeners: these are the extreme type; people who even garden in the cold of winter! They could be a source of information as well as a great source to help you start your own seed bank if they are devoted to open-pollinated seeds. They often have more seeds in one season than they could possibly grow.

Open-pollinated seeds are a great way to start conserving and expanding our vegetable species' diversity. You do more than just grow the beets and beans.

It is important to store these properly when saving your own seeds. If not stored properly, not only is it a waste of time and resources to save the seeds, but it is also necessary to make sure that your seeds are viable when it comes to planting them!

Below are just a few tips on seed storage, bearing in mind the location/climate factors in storage, as well as available space, what types of seeds you are saving/storing, and how long you want the seeds to be stored; make sure to save the seeds at full maturity.

To dry the seeds, put them in a cool, dry place — do not leave them outside where they can be influenced by the elements. Placing the seeds on paper bags helps draw out and soak up moisture.

Place these in glass mason jars or baby food jars with tight lids once the seeds are completely dry. I prefer to use containers for baby food since they are small and simple to transport if necessary.

Many people would buy small packets of silica to put the seeds in the jars to remove any remaining moisture. It is not mandatory if you live in a dry area, but if you live in a humid or damp area, I would suggest it.

The seeds are always stored in a cold, dry spot. You should put them in your refrigerator if you want them to last longer. When you do this, use the silica packets for sure, and make sure the lids are clean and secure.

Some seeds will survive for up to five years, but I would suggest that the saved seeds be checked at the start of each growing season to ensure that they remain viable. Date your bottles, so you know when the seeds have been saved. If the seeds are over five years old, I'm not going to put a lot of stock into them being viable, so it's probably time to save some new seeds of that type.

THE COMPLETE GUIDE TO GROWING AND STORING VEGETABLES, FRUITS, HERBS AND FLOWERS SEEDS

Everyone has vegetables listed in their diets. It is recommended that we should consume vegetables daily. It is fun to grow and eat vegetables by yourself. But the question arises of how vegetables should be grown. We will also see some tips and suggestions on how vegetables are grown.

If you're talking about how to grow vegetables in your yard, then it's not that hard. Growing vegetables demand plenty of sunshine. So, you need to see if your garden is receiving enough sunshine. Start in spring and getting a vegetable garden near the kitchen is always better. In this way, you have easy access to the garden which would allow faster planting. The seeds must be soaked and require humidity. They are ready to grow, once they're a little plump. Many vegetables like broccoli and cabbage don't need you to soak their seeds. The process of overdoing the soaking could damage the seeds. But don't throw them away too quickly.

When considering how to grow vegetables in the cold, you'll need to use tepees that are filled with water around the tender vegetables. There are other plastic sheets available on the market that serve as a barrier to the plant until it is filled with water. Also, the sun can easily move through this sheet so the plants stay warm longer. You should be planting them deep inside the earth.

If you are wondering how to grow vegetables that grow on vines. If you plant them in your garden, they may not grow the way you want them to and they may grow into the rest of your yard. But if they are rooted more deeply, then they will easily maintained. Tomatoes require horizontal planting into the trench. So, the seed doesn't have to be sown deep in the soil; it will grow well.

Try to avoid cutworms that spoil delicate, tender plants. It will save space when planting vegetable plants if you always try to position them vertically. It is possible to allow vegetables such as cucumber, beans, melons, etc. to grow on trees or walls, rather than being scattered around them. Both the vegetables need timely fertilizers. Ensure to take good care of them. It will mean they continue to offer vegetables at regular intervals.

The method can be a lot smoother overall than you would expect. There are also some factors involved in growing plants in your vegetable gardens that you may not have previously known. The resulting experience can be both enjoyable and satisfying once you know the main guiding points.

Here are the secret to getting good plants. It's important that every plant gets what it needs. Around the same time, we need to protect the plants from the stuff they don't need. This consistency is what makes division so vital to success. Find one of the most important plant needs: water. One plant may require substantially more water than another. Home gardens are supplied with water either by rain or direct watering. Try to keep plants with similar water requirements close together. This way, when applied, there's less concern about where the water will go. The landscape may be more important in the case of rain. Plants requiring little water should be planted in proper soil to allow drainage, while in some instances, plants needing more water should be accommodated by proper soil selection and other means. Your planting needs include much of how to grow vegetable garden plants, but there is another dimension to a garden that should not be overlooked.

Plants are not single-minded. We hold the capacity for interaction. You may have learned the story of the cross-pollinated plants. Maybe you also met someone who blended flavors in plants growing next to each other. That is the second reason to separate properly. There are a variety of plants that can pollinate throughout. If you're going to allow the plants to grow and evolve through a natural cycle, then study the plants you want. In certain cases, you may decide to use neutral plants to distinguish interacting plants. In certain situations, you may be expected to leave a bare spot in your garden. However, usually, there is something that can be planted at that bare spot.

Considering the above, you should have a very good but simple understanding of how to grow plants in a vegetable garden. That does not mean your garden has to be the same year after year. There are one or two spots in several gardens that are rotated from year to year. This adds variety to the growing vegetables but in some cases, they may also increase the soil quality of the garden. The combinations are endless and can bring even more excitement to the gardening experience. That also means you'll have to share more fascinating vegetables with others. The smiles will continue, encouraging those who actually eat the vegetables to engage in the garden. They might not be fond of weeding but many will enjoy watering and other nursing activities.

Growing vegetables is also fun. It takes time to prepare the soil and do the actual planting but it's worth the effort to be able to select a fresh tomato or cucumber for a salad. Saving on the grocery bill whenever possible is always a plus. It's not complicated but growing a vegetable garden takes a little know-how.

You can grow the vegetables in two ways. You can grow them in the conventional outdoor greenhouse, or you can grow them in containers. No matter which gardening approach you select, a sunny location is the one constant to both. If you have trees in your yard, trimming the trees can increase the amount of sun the garden area gets. You would be able to push them around and be in the sun for longer periods of time depending on the size and weight of the containers.

Knowing how to cultivate a vegetable garden to achieve full success

Container gardening is great for growing vegetables if there isn't a lot of room in the yard. Many of the vegetables that can be grown in containers are tomatoes, eggplant, peppers, and squash. Some vegetables need a minimum container of one gallon, and some need a larger amount. Compost filled containers are best designed for container gardening. Vegetables may begin with seeds. Plant the seeds in a warm spot, so that they are ready for transplanting once the season begins. Starter plants can also be purchased from the nearest gardening centre.

You may want to create in your yard a traditional vegetable garden. Choose a place where sun abounds for a large part of the day. Measure the area your garden has available and calculate the square footage. There are two reasons why the area is important. One, to know how much fertilizer or mulch may be required and two, to decide how many plants can be planted.

When the soil has been prepared and fertilized, according to the instructions, plant seeds or starter plants.

Overcrowding your garden won't let the plants grow properly and you'll end up with no or little vegetables. Depending on the crop, germination can take from a week to six weeks not matter where you plant seeds. When planting starter plants, it will take them a few days to develop and they will look wilted. Water the crop, or seeds, after planting. The soil should be moist but not too wet.

Containers should have holes in the bottom to allow drainage and they should be placed on bricks or blocks. They should be placed in a graded yard lawn, so the water does not settle. If it rains, then water is not needed. Water not with a stream of water but with a gentle spray. Try setting up a sprinkler in the garden on a watering day for a few hours.

KEEPING THE GARDEN FREE FROM RABBITS

That would need regular weeding. When weeds are allowed to take root in the garden, they will consume the energy from the soil and leave the plants with little to no energy. Your garden may need a fence or some other barrier to keep out the critters.

How to grow a vegetable garden means you need to learn what your plants need to thrive. So, don't worry about your new vegetable planting, I will guide you through the whole process. Let's go over the basics you will need to get your garden ready.

-- Clear the field, and make sure it's perfect for growing your vegetables. How do you know whether it's suitable or not? Well just make sure you rake it clean so there's no leaves or weeds around to hinder your garden's production.

-- First, you'll want to till the soil and really break it down so your garden can breathe properly.

-- After the soil is tilled and broken down, the fertilizer you intend to use will be added.

-- After the fertilizer has been applied, you will have to till the soil again to blend the fertilizer, so that it can work to its maximum potential.

First, apply a little water to the soil. Don't place a lot of water; make sure none of the water is still at the edge.

Learning how to grow a vegetable garden will initially be a process of trial and error, so don't panic if you screw up the first time around. When you add too much water, then just wait a couple of days and try again.

-- You are now able to start planting after the water has been applied and when the soil is moist and there is none settling

See, look how easy that was. Now, your first little vegetable garden has a spaced cleared out and ready. Now the fun part is really starting. You'll have to go get your desired seeds at your local nursery.

Cucumbers and melons are able to grow easily in compost. Some leftover food and fruit used to fertilize them. It will as manure, and will help the crop to grow well. It is the safest way of growing those vegetables.

There's a huge array of vegetables you can easily grow in your backyard. When you've laid out your plot and determined what to grow, now it's time to populate your plot and begin to grow. However, it is not enough just to plant vegetable plants into the garden and wait for them to bring fresh produce. Different vegetables grow under various conditions and some need more nutrients than others. Here are some useful tips from just a few popular varieties to get the best from.

Peas

The sound of a juicy fat pea pod bursting open to expose the first few peas of the year is pleasurable. For me, peas are the sweets of the world, and it's a wonder that anyone ever makes it back to my kitchen! Make sure you dig the soil well when growing peas, and put in plenty of manure before planting because peas love rich moisture-retaining soil. Mulching around each plant's base and frequent watering will also benefit them through dry weather spells which they hate. Lastly, outside sowing will depend upon your location but will usually be between early and mid-spring. But first make sure the soil's warmed up enough. Peas should be well supported with sticks or stakes, allowing for good space on the plants for the pods to grow. Peas are a favorite among birds so covering young plants with chicken wire or plastic netting may be a smart idea. Harvest the pods periodically to ensure that they are as fresh as possible and use or freeze as needed.

Runner beans

I will recommend to those with little experience growing vegetables to grow runner beans. They grow quickly and require little effort. They look amazing and have a long harvest time, yielding a big crop. There are only three main requirements for runner beans – deeply dug soil, lots of well-rotted manure and lots of water. You need a strong support network for growing runner beans. High bamboo obelisks or firm sticks will make the perfect climbing structure. Make sure you put your stakes in early and protect them well – how heavy these plants can become when they're loaded with beans is incredible! Sow the seeds indoors in early to mid-spring and the young plants can then be planted out in early summer at the bottom of any upright support. When they hit the top of the support structure, pinch the rising tips out, so the plants don't get top-heavy. Choose the pods when they're young and may be stringy until they swell like older pods.

Tomatoes

The tangy-sweet taste of fresh tomatoes straight from the vine is quite enjoyable. Tomatoes can be grown in your greenhouse, in a growbag or in a yard. I tend to grow them in the greenhouse because a better crop is guaranteed as the plants are not so dependent on the environment. Don't bother growing seed tomatoes, they can be fiddly, and you still end up with many more plants than you can use or give way. Gardener's pleasure is a favorite of mine. This variety yields an abundance of very sweet and juicy, tiny cherry tomatoes. Pinch the growing tip of plants out once five or six healthy-looking fruit-bearing side shoots have been produced. Water well and feed your tomatoes and they'll reward you for the entire summer.

Potatoes

Vegetable gardeners claims that potatoes are an easy crop to grow that can be relied on to produce a successful harvest. If you do not have the space to grow both early and maincrop varieties then my advice will be to stick to early varieties of salad. None is more rewarding than digging up the first salad potatoes in summer and eating them with a nice butter dollop. Seed potatoes need chitting before planting them; that is they are sprouting short green shoots. Begin planting potatoes early through mid-spring. The safest way to dig a trench is around it. Grip each potato carefully so that no shoots are knocked off. Plant to a depth of about 15 cm, with 30 cm between each potato. If the shoots emerge above the ground, start the earthing-up cycle by raking the soil around them and over them to create a ridge. This prevents the tuber from being exposed to light and turning green which makes them toxic. Water young plants well to ensure strong tuber cultivation. Watch out for potato blight which, in warm wet summers, can be a particular problem and can ruin a crop. Harvesting the first potatoes is like making a treasure search. When the plants have flowered, the crop is ready. Choose a moist, dry day and scrape a bit of the soil away to test if the tubers are large enough. Leave the tubers exposed to the air to allow them to dry off for a few hours. This makes its handling easier.

Carrots

Ever wonder why one would bother to grow carrots when they are fairly cheap to buy and store well? Yet I don't think you've really tasted a carrot until you ate one you've grown yourself. The flavor is so much stronger and sweeter. Carrots can be sown regularly from March to July, but don't start too early as the soil has to be warm for effective germination. Carrots are a vegetable that does not like being transplanted and must thus be sown directly into the soil. Carrots need a soft, well-drained soil, free of obstructions, to avoid club or twisted root formation. Therefore, growing them in broad garden with free-draining sealed compost or soil is often more effective. Sow carrot seed thinly but this can be difficult as the seeds are very small, so expect the seedlings to thin out once they emerge. Beware of carrot flying in early summer. Consider growing chives next to your carrots, as the chives' scent is good enough to hide the carrots' scent that attracts the fly. Keep the carrots in the field until the last possible moment. When harvested, the fresher they are, the better they taste!

HOW TO GROW VEGETABLES IN WINTER

The majority of people believe the vegetable growing season ends in September and begins in April or May. Although this could be the time with the most comfortable temperatures – where you can spend more time outdoors – winter is not a "dead season."

In addition to preparing your soil for the coming spring, you can also practice winter planting and keep on growing vegetables. I'm going to write about two key points in this article: using seasonal extenders to prolong the "warmer" season and growing crops in winter to harvest in spring.

Why do I keep growing plants when they get cold?

For winter gardening, you can use the so-called "season extenders" to retain some degree of warmth for your plants and protect them from wind and snow damage. This can be:

- You can create small row covers that are only large enough to cover your plants; or you can create some form of greenhouses that you can enter and work in.

In addition, the benefits of these systems are that you use the greenhouse effect to heat the air under the respective cover. However, when it gets cold at night, cold-resistant plants do grow best.

When you use greenhouse vegetable planting plans, vegetables can be grown at just about any time of year. Growing them in a hothouse is similar to growing garden vegetables in the summer. You just need to take a few extra measures to artificially supply what they would experience in a normal situation.

You can use two methods to grow the vegetables in a portable greenhouse. Throughout the day, the first uses the energy of the sun to heat up the system, which is called the cold process. When the temperature drops, a heating system turns on to hold the temperature at least 45 degrees F.

Plants do not flourish with this technique but rather are only maintained until they can be put outdoors in the summer.

Growing vegetables in winter need water, so the approach to use is a warm technique. Garden greenhouses need to maintain a minimum temperature of 55 degrees F to expand and require a heating unit. Heating devices can be natural, propane, or electric.

Within a greenhouse nearly every vegetable that you can grow outside can be grown inside. Nearly every vegetable has a variety to grow indoors that have been hybridized. For most catalogs, you will find them seeds that can be sown in the winter. The seed types that you want are those that don't need much heat to develop. You will look for varieties that grow small or can be trimmed to be small because, in one of these systems, there is not as much space as in a yard.

Pollination is an essential natural activity which has to be carried out artificially. Unfortunately, insects do not dwell within, particularly bees. Pollinating tomatoes provides an example of pollinating a vegetable. Tomato vines should be attached to stakes made of bamboo, and the stakes should be tapped in the morning and in the evening when the flower is ready. You'll know that when the petals start curving backward, the flor is finished. Pay careful attention to this, as the flowers can contain pollen only for three days to pollinate the crop.

Since there isn't much sunshine in the winter, you have to incorporate sunshine by using heat lamps. Most of the vegetables need a minimum of eight hours a day. The plants would of course still need to be periodically watered and fertilized.

Winter greenhouse gardening is a little more difficult and takes longer than summer, but it is also satisfying. On a snowy day in January, you can go to the greenhouse and select a tomato ripened on the vine. Any time of year, you can have the complete taste of summer.

Season planting crops are available that can be planted even in late fall or winter months (also when the field is frozen). In fact, some plants (so-called cold season plants) are intended to be planted more and if planted late in the year, do not grow as well.

The benefit of early planting is that

a.) you get good, resistant plants and
b.) you get your vegetable yields much sooner (in spring, rather than in summer).

You should also clear your beds of all dead plant material (also autumn foliage) before planting any seeds, crack the ground open, apply compost and till it in. You can use organic fertilizers if your soil was heavily cultivated in the previous year.

Typical cold/hardy plants are as follows:

Tubers and roots should not be grown early in the year because they can quickly rot from wetness. Nevertheless, if you combine the two tips cold covers and cold seasonal plants, you can even grow potatoes before their time is due, and transplant them into your "natural" beds once the weather becomes warm again.

I hope that information will inspire you to try to garden yourself in winter.

AQUAPONICS-HOW TO GROW

VEGETABLES QUICKLY

Aquaponics - How to Create and Operate a Setup

This is the most important question that emerged when we consider raising fish and vegetables side by side. Aquaponics is also the art of growing vegetables as well as fish using very little resources – mainly water already present in your fish tank. In short, the idea of using the waste that comes from your fishponds is to supply your vegetables with nutrients.

This is both relatively easy and a totally organic way to grow your favorite vegetables without thinking about soil cultivation or fertilization, not to mention the use of toxic synthetic fertilizers. You just need to feed the fish in an aquaponics system, and you might even cultivate your own fish food.

Aquaponics - How to use the new fish tank?

Before delving into the Aquaponics information, let us see how the water from your fish tank is useful for growing vegetables. We all know that fish generate a lot of waste, which produces ammonia, which, if left to build-up, is toxic to the fish (a big reason why we need to refresh the water in a normal setup at regular intervals unless there is an appropriate filter system in place). The plants do the filtering at an aquaponics facility. The plants, however, cannot make use of ammonia. What happens is that bacteria in the tank water will grow naturally, and they will convert the ammonia into nitrates. The nitrates act as a natural fertilizer for all types of vegetables, thereby providing a unique opportunity to grow fresh vegetables with the help of the fish's natural waste.

Research has shown that growing plants using water from fish tanks makes the vegetables grow at fifty percent faster than average. Also, you get the chance to see your favorite vegetables grow in a very short time. That isn't all. Now the same water can be recycled back to the filtered fish tank and therefore keep the fish alive in a healthy environment.

Aquaponics – How to get started:

The basic process of beginning with Aquaponics is very simple. For plants to grow, you need fishponds and reservoirs. There are ready-built kits available on the market, though your system can be easily designed and produced. Whatever you do, the simple answer you need to know about how to get started with aquaponics is:

1. What you intend to grow
2. Existing room,
3. The kind of system that you want to create.

Once developed, aquaponics doesn't take much of your time to care for. The fish tanks are still at a lower level than the rising beds, whichever method you use because the water from the beds will naturally flow back into the fish tanks. Recall that the water is recycled and that is why aquaponics only use about 2 percent of the amount of water that would be used in your home garden.

You would need a pump to bring a set amount of water into the beds so that the plants still get a proper amount of water with the nutrients they need and send it back to the tank filtered. In certain processes, the plant roots remain immersed in the mud, while the mud is drained into the plants.

Aquaponics is useful in three ways: you get fresh vegetables, you get fresh fish, and you're going to save a little money.

Aquaponics is particularly suitable for areas with very little water supply, as it requires very little water. Helping to provide the much-needed food would be particularly acceptable in third world countries. It is also very useful for us to learn how to set up an aquaponics system because it will give us cheap fresh vegetables and cheap fresh fish. Especially when the price of vegetables goes sky high because of weather conditions.

How to Raise Year-round Vegetables With Indoor Aquaponics

By using aquaponics to build your own indoor greenhouse, you will no longer have to think about paying the ridiculous winter price for fresh vegetables. Alternatively, right in your basement or spare bedroom, you can grow your vegetables year-round. Think about something new! Maybe the best thing about it is the fact that you would have firsthand knowledge of what you are eating.

If you're not acquainted with aquaponics, let me quickly get you up to speed. Aquaponics is essentially a hydroponic extension — the art of raising plants without the use of dirt or soil. Roots of the plant rest directly in a water bath. In general, the plant itself is in a floating form of bed. With hydroponics, to feed the plants, you had to add nutrients to the water.

The plants are getting their nutrients in a much more sustainable and organic way with aquaponics – from raising fish. If you've ever had fish before, you know they can put out some gross by-products like ammonia and so on. Okay, here's where we see in practice the great circle of life—those nasty by-products are just what plants need to grow. Therefore, the fish emulsion feeds the plants, and they filter the water for the fish as the plants take what they need from the water. This is an all-natural, and all organic process.

If you wonder what kind of plants you can grow with aquaponics — well, there's basically something going on. Beginners may want to start out with a green leafy veggie like lettuce. Growth is usually the fastest. Certain plants you can add include basil, watercress, peas, tomatoes, red and green peppers, strawberries and melons as you get the hang of it. You can try many things. The true test of whether a plant works for you or not is just to try and see.

Aquaponic planting has another advantage. You get to eat the fish, too! When you're looking for a way to become sustainable (or off the grid), this type of garden will not only give you fresh fruit and veggies throughout the year but also protein. This is from the comfort of your own house.

You probably think it would be expensive to have an indoor aquaponic gardening program, right? Okay, yeah, if you are buying a ready-made device that's possibly real. The good news is that it's totally possible to develop your device with a good DIY guide. Your commodity bills' savings will cover the operating expenses. Moreover, you get the added advantage of understanding where the food of your family comes from and whether it is actually safe.

HOW TO GROW VEGETABLES IN CONTAINERS

The benefits of growing vegetables in containers are numerous. Maintaining the soil is better. There are also more choices for dealing with changes in light and temperature. Management of the pests is therefore easier. Whether inside a home, on the patio, or in a greenhouse, container gardening is possible.

Some vegetables take up large quantities of space, such as pumpkins and cucumber, but they should do well in containers. Peas, peppers, carrots, and tomatoes do just as well when grown in a container, if not better.

It is important to pick a container large enough for a fully grown, harvest-ready plant. Choose soil that is free from weeds and will be sure to add ample fertilizer before planting. Consider the synthetic soil-like material, or peat moss mixtures, wood chips, and perlite for specific species.

Be sure to prepare the soil or use a synthetic medium before planting. It makes control of the water much easier. To keep the container-grown plants safe, it is necessary to balance adequate drainage and good moisture retention. Place some marbles at the bottom of the container to avoid the clogging of holes and ensure proper drainage. Mix the clay particles into industrial soil prepared for planting.

Also, if the soil is well prepared, water carefully. If containers are close to a window, soil will dry out quickly. Through overwatering, it is easy to introduce root rot or to forget that watering chores have been completed, so keep a soil moisture tester nearby.

For most situations, the purchase of professionally prepared container planting soil is simpler. Soil straight from the outside is not normally a good choice for container development. Nature has a way to remove water from clay-like dry soils. The water retention of clay is exacerbated when used in a container and can contribute to root rot.

Many vegetables require sunlight. You can anticipate a great tomato crop if you are growing it on a windowsill facing south which receives several hours of sunlight every day. Tomato plants often grow in the sun, so burning them is a low risk. Other plants, such as spinach, prefer less direct sunlight. Place these partially in shade. When you're using planting containers, it's easy to place your plants in different weather conditions.

Whether your plants are sitting outdoors, or are kept indoors, pests will reach them. Use an insect screen, as you would in an outdoor garden. Larvae may grow in container plant soil if the eggs were laid in the soil before they were planted. When used in compliance with standards, insecticide soaps and other commercial mixtures are suitable for plant handling, and good for you while consuming plants.

Having readily available fresh vegetables gives you convenience and safe eating options. While container gardening takes some effort, the time and commitment are well worth the rewards.

Growing fruits and vegetables in containers is easy, even for a beginner, and if you don't have a big garden, it can be a good idea. There are many varieties of vegetables suitable for growing in this way, including green onions, eggplant, cabbage, cucumbers, green beans, and tomatoes, perhaps the most frequently grown. Some of these are climbing plants so some support like wooden posts, trellis or wire cages will be required. Containers can be put on patios, balconies or anywhere you have a moist, suitable room.

What varieties of vegetables are sufficient to grow in containers?

It is not possible to grow all varieties of these vegetables in containers, and you will usually have to select dwarf varieties, often called "mini veg" or defined as "appropriate for close spacing." For beans, pick a variety like Hestia or the Sutton, for Balconi, Patio, Sweet 1000 or Tiny Tim tomatoes. Often ideal are California Wonder Peppers, and Minnesota Midget Melons. Try Little Gem, or Tom Thumb for lettuces. All of these varieties take up less space than the standard varieties and were specially designed for growing in confined spaces.

What type of container would you select?

It is possible to use almost any sort of container, just make sure it is wide enough and has plenty of holes in the drainage. In hanging baskets, other types of tomatoes grow very well. Terracotta pots are beautiful but require more care than plastic pots because they appear to dry out much more quickly. If possible, pick a light-colored pot because it is cooler in the hotter months and hold heat less than dark-colored pots so the soil won't overheat too quickly. To help save water use a drip tray under the containers.

What places are ideal for vegetable containers?

You can place your pots on a balcony or patio but make sure they're going to be in the heat for most of the day. To grow well, vegetables will need a minimum of six hours of sunshine a day. In colder climates, putting them against a wall facing south is a smart idea. You could also place the pots on a mobile platform so you can move them around to get sunlight from every direction; that will lead to more even growth and allow you to move them out of the sun in the heat of the day.

How do you plant your container of vegetables?

You'll need to use a decent quality potting compost. For container growing, ordinary garden soil is not recommended because it does not have the right nutrient balance and may contain pests and weed seed. You may buy the vegetables as young transplants, or you can cultivate them from seed indoors or in a greenhouse. Place a bit of mulch on top of the soil until they are transplanted to your pots to help preserve moisture. You may use mold or straw for the root. Don't crowd the seedlings; give them plenty of space to develop and install a structure where they can climb if necessary.

How much are you expected to water your vegetable containers?

Most containers would require watering every day and you could apply three or four times a week to a low nutrient solution. Do not spray directly on the plants as spraying on the leaves may promote mold and fungi around its bases. Don't let the pots get waterlogged but make sure that the drainage is sufficient.

It's fun growing vegetables in containers and it's very easy even for a beginner gardener. Once you harvest your crop of fresh vegetables, ready to cook or add to the salad, you'll be well rewarded.

How to create an Elevated Bed Vegetable Garden

If you're thinking of building an elevated bed vegetable garden, there are some important things to bear in mind. Your garden layout that is the most important thing to consider.

Many first-time gardeners also make the mistake of designing a garden that is much harder to care for than they thought at first. Using the right amount of nutrients, water and sunshine, choosing the best layout for your raised bed will mean less work for you along with extra benefits for your vegetables. This, of course, is down to a few extra items, so here are a few simple tips to help you build the perfect layout.

Planning ahead: this is the first thing to do, and one of the most important when thinking about having a vegetable garden on a raised bed. Doing so would mean that it is set up properly so that at a later date, you do not have to switch items around. When you have left the right amount of space, you can expand later. This also affects the available space, so you need to think about which vegetables you wish to grow.

You'll benefit a lot from using separate boxes for every vegetable. It is something you need to be careful about while planning your project. With each vegetable, the reason for using different boxes is that some will require special care (this means you'll have other boxes for the more vulnerable plants).

One thing you can't forget is choosing the appropriate position for your beds. No matter what size of bed you use, it's important to have the best spot. The best positions will include:

- Clear ground
- Highest quantity of sunlight
- Good ventilation. You need to avoid beds that are too wide, making a wide elevated bed will make maintenance difficult. The ideal size will be about 4 feet long for your raised vegetable garden beds. This means that access from both sides is relatively easy.

You want to make sure the taller plants are at the back when planting your raised bed. The reason for doing so is that these plants won't block the sunlight for the smaller plants.

It's a lot of fun to build your new, raised bed vegetable garden. So, having all these tips in mind will make sure your new raised bed garden is a success along with being exciting for everyone concerned. Then, soon enough, you'll reap the benefits of getting your own vegetable garden built in your home.

What problems are solved by an elevated bed vegetable garden?

A lot of people have concerns about growing your vegetables. They have heard of different styles of garden designs and are searching for a guide to help them get started with growing vegetables without much trouble. One question you might ask is: what are the problems of managing a raised bed vegetable garden? Let's examine some of the common problems facing gardeners, and what solutions can be solved with this kind.

COMMON VEGETABLE GARDENING PROBLEMS

When it comes to having a vegetable garden started, those who want to grow their vegetables are often faced with four common problems. These relate to:

1. Space issues
2. Poor soil quality
3. Drainage issues
4. Accessibility issues

Now that we are aware of the four key problems vegetable gardeners have to deal with let's see if we can solve each. The difficulty of growing vegetables can be summed up by considering the construction of an elevated bed vegetable garden for those who must deal with these kinds of struggles.

- • Space issues – Most people live in subdivisions or city blocks, all of which appear to have little space in their yards. You can grow enough vegetables for home use in a garden that is elevated above the ground using a limited amount of room only. A garden bed that is 2 feet by 10 feet should yield enough vegetables for your family.

- • Poor soil quality – There are many areas that have too much sand or clay and others that don't have enough or too many natural soil nutrients to grow well, including alkaline. With a raised bed vegetable garden, the plants are above ground level and you select the soil mix from which the bed is filled. Along with other soil mixtures, you can thus incorporate organic growing materials.

- • Drainage issues – Many yards just don't drain well. Trying to grow your own vegetables in soil that is not properly draining can deprive your plants of the oxygen that is vital to their existence. Bad drainage can also contribute to the creation of diseases due to the excessively saturated soil that can damage your plants. Because the vegetables are well above ground level with proper drainage outlets as you build the bed, having a raised bed garden can eliminate this problem.

- • Accessibility issues – Accessibility to the plants they cultivate can be an issue for some people. Elevated bed gardens can be built on pedestals fully off the ground so that the bed height can accommodate without having to bend or kneel like a typical garden would require. This approach may benefit those with physical disabilities who are interested in growing vegetables but have not been able to do so before but they can now reach their plants. In this form of garden design, you are also not expected to walk through rows so tending and harvesting your crops will just be a short distance away.

These are only a couple of the problems a raised bed vegetable garden can overcome. For several gardening enthusiasts, this garden design is becoming increasingly popular. It's an economically sound measure to grow your own vegetables and a healthy activity to get involved in. Now that you know how the problems having a raised bed vegetable garden bed can solve, isn't it time for you to have one?

Modern vegetable gardens need a large amount of hard work and care – weeding, feeding and strict planting schedules. There is also the seasonality issue, which allows beds to rest during the cooler months, producing nothing at all. Instead, we are told to plant crops of green manure, apply inorganic fertilizers and chemicals to improve soil quality. It takes a lot of energy, effort and year-round commitment in using the conventional way of growing your own food.

But does that really need to be so hard?

Let me ask you this question. Should a forest ponder how to grow? Does it take to turn in its soil every season? Will anyone come along every so often and take pH samples or plant seeds? Can it weed or spray dangerous chemicals?

Clearly not!

Modern methods of vegetable gardening concentrate on the issues. Did you note that books about gardening are full of ways to fix problems? For several years, I was a conventional gardener and I noticed that the solution to most of the problems actually created a new set of problems. In other words, the problem with the issues is that it creates more problems.

Let's look at a common traditional gardening practice, and I'll show you how one problem can escalate into a whole host of issues.

Imagine a traditional vegetable garden which is planted with rows of different vegetables. Bare patches between the vegetables are fairly large. A bare patch to a typical gardener is merely a bare patch. But a bare patch is an empty niche space, for an ecologist is an empty niche and is literally an invitation for other life forms to take up residence. Nature does not accept empty niche spaces and weeds are the most productive fillers of a niche space. In ecological terms, which is what a weed is – a niche space filler. Weeds are plants that colonize very well. They wouldn't be called weeds if they didn't.

Now back to our plot. Weeds are forming in empty void spaces. Quite often, too many weeds are to be picked individually, so the typical gardener uses a hoe to drive them into the dirt. In many gardening books, even in organic gardening books, I have read that your hoe is your best friend.

So, the message that we get is that using a hoe is the answer to a problem.

But I want to show you how using a hoe is actually creating a new set of problems. Firstly, turning soil excites weed seeds and produces a new weed explosion. Then, second, soil turning upsets the ecosystem of soil. Generally, the top layer of soil is dry and without structure. By turning it up, you put deeper organized soil on the surface and beneath the structureless soil. The band of structureless soil widened over time. Structureless soil has much less ability to retain moisture, meaning that the garden now needs more water to keep the plants alive.

Besides this issue, structureless soil cannot pass its nutrients on to the plants as effectively as possible. The garden needs to use fertilizer now as well. Most fertilizers destroy soil biology, which is very important to create soil structure and the supply of plant nutrients. Eventually, the soil is a dead material that doesn't have the required nutrient balance to produce fully established foods. The diet would, in turn, be deficient in vitamins and minerals. This topic has already arisen in modern-day farming. According to Dr Tim Lobstein, Food Commission Director, "Agriculture today does not require the soil to enrich itself, but depends on artificial fertilizers that do not substitute the large range of nutrient plants and human needs." During the past 60 years, commercially produced foods have undergone substantial nutrient and mineral content reductions."

Could you see how we began with the weed issue but ended up with the new problems of lower capacity for water keeping and infertile soils? Finally, we have the potentially serious issue of rising low nutrient content foods. Modern gardening methods often try only to repair the problem, not the cause.

There's one solution, though! We need to use a technique that combines pest ecology, plant ecology, soil ecology and crop management into a system that addresses the causes of these problems. That technique must be sufficiently efficient to be economically viable. However, it should be able to produce enough food to compete against conventional techniques, per given area.

For many years, I have been researching an ecologically-based method of growing food. This approach uses zero tillage, zero pesticides, has minimal weeds and requires a fraction of physical effort (compared to conventional cultivation of vegetables). It also produces multiple times more, per area, and provides food each day of the year.

My ecological garden imitates nature in such a way that the garden looks like a natural ecosystem and behaves like it. Succession layering of plants (as we see in natural ecosystems) provides efficient control of diseases. It also removes, of course, the need for crop rotation, rest beds or green manure crops. Soil conservation is approached in a natural way and the result is that year after year the structure and fertility of the soil becomes richer and richer. A further benefit of this method is automatic self-seeding regeneration. It happens naturally as dormant seeds germinate; with attractive plants filling vacant niche spaces, not weeds.

Unfortunately, the biggest challenge facing this approach is to persuade conventional gardeners of its advantages. The gardening industry, like other businesses, is trapped in doing things in a certain way. The ecologically-based approach needs such little human involvement that many people would, in my view, be irritated by the lack of need to monitor what is happening. Of course, people love taking charge of their lives, but with this approach, you allow nature to take the reins. It is a test of faith in natural laws that are very basic. Such natural rules, however, are 100 percent accurate in my experience.

One reason typical reason gardener do not like this approach is that it eliminates all the mysticism of being an expert. You see, that method is so easy that any person can do it under any circumstances, anywhere in the world. For a seasoned gardener, when an embarrassingly easy solution comes along, it can actually be very threatening.

I have no doubt this is the way we are going to produce food in the future. It's just sort of common sense. Why wouldn't we use a system with a fraction of the effort, which produces several times more food? I know it will take some time to persuade people that growing food is actually very instinctual and straightforward, but people will accept the approach with patience and proper explanation.

Clever Ways to Achieve Natural Pest Control in Your Vegetable Garden

When you're someone who can't deal with a bunch of artificial chemicals invading your vegetable garden, the whole gardening activity is especially challenging. Yet it doesn't have to be so. If you happen to be a gardener who likes things to be normal and who loves toying around with nontraditional methods of preserving his crop, there are some common-sense solutions on offer.

Fashioning all kinds of new natural pest control contraptions doesn't take long, getting in the right counter-predatory steps and using organic approaches to your problem. It takes patience and some sort of pleasure to see how nature can be used to tackle some of the issues it creates.

Let's get first with a kind of insect that doesn't trouble your plants so much as it makes you toil away in the heat of summer weeding, digging and planting at your greenhouse – we're talking about flies and wasps, of course. But gardeners wouldn't worry too much about their personal bother that if they weren't too bad for their plants. Support is at hand with an innovative concept in a simple wasp trap that you can also make from empty soda bottles. What you need is a few clear plastic bottles with removed labels, filled with a little thick sweet syrup at the bottom. All sorts of insects won't be able to resist the sweet and will be utterly confused about how to make their way out. This is such a popular approach that they render even decorative bottles with stands and other needs for positioning.

Organic pesticides exist for pests that are not attracted by sweet syrup, which may aid you in your search for natural pest control. What gardeners are using is that which is called diatomaceous earth. It's mix with water, and spray all over their garden, particularly over branches of flowering plants. The poisonous diatomaceous earth that appears to corrode them will scare away visiting insects. The only problem with these is that this way too can turn away friendly garden insects such as butterflies and ladybugs.

Natural methods of pest control also work with larger rodents, such as rabbits. Have you ever tried to create a vegetable garden with some rabbits around? They believe that this is a buffet set up for them. The best way to keep the rabbits or deer out of your vegetable patches will be to use chicken or rabbit wire designed wire cages. You build yourself a cage to fit over any patch of vegetables and you should be okay. Planting garlic all around your vegetable garden would be a better way though. Many animals dislike the scent as do other humans. It's just a very clever way to stop animals from coming in and feeling there's something tasty there for them.

IMPORTANT TOOLS THAT ARE USEFUL

FOR VEGETABLE GARDENING

If you're a keen gardener and want to grow your own vegetables, there's a wide variety of resources available that can help you produce some award-winning. If you're an accomplished vegetable gardener, you'll appreciate the value of getting the right equipment to successfully do the work. Once you head out to buy all of your vegetable patch gardening equipment, it's important to think about the scale of your vegetable garden and the physical ability to do the job that vegetable gardening demands.

The first step in vegetable gardening is to plot out your patch of vegetables and to till the soil to ensure it is ready for seeding. Especially, if you have a large vegetable garden, this can be very intensive work. There's a variety of tools to support you. A spade and a fork are the first two tools you'll need for this work. The spade is useful for digging up the area of soil you have marked out for your crops, while the fork can be used to further split the soil into small, more suitable chunks and add some compost to the mix. If you think you may have trouble digging; however, it may be worth investing in a growers' machine or a rotary tiller. A rotary tiller or cultivator will do all the hard work and dig up the land area for you to transform the soil as desired.

After you've tilled your soil, you need to think about seeding. Most times it's a good idea to go over the soil with a rake to smooth it out and prepare it, so sewing your seed choices is perfect enough for you. It's a good idea to put your vegetables in sets and leave ample space between them.

Online sales of vegetable seeds can be a very good option. Many companies don't package their seeds in advance, which allows the seeds to remain fresh longer. Likewise, several retailers will ship the next day, so fast delivery is guaranteed. You'll also find a very large variety of seeds you could not find at your local store. Also, greenhouses or nurseries do not have a comprehensive array of viable seed options for vegetables. If you're searching for the rare organic tomato seed, you'll probably be able to find it online.

Most vegetable seed companies offer some kind of guarantee online. Some say they will refund your purchase price or substitute the item if a seed does not perform within a given time frame. This is the most popular form of guarantee that you'll encounter. Other assurances claim if you are not happy for any reason, they will refund your money. Regardless, make sure you understand the terms and conditions before you buy.

Prices are typically very similar, so check out a few items before you buy them. See how many you can actually get. Many sites may be less costly because they can sell a lighter weight. Be mindful of the seed price, as well. For example, seeds made from heirloom produce the best tomato degustations. There are several different forms of the same herb, as well. Verify that you compare the exact same crop, or you won't get an accurate picture.

Have an idea of what sort of vegetables you want to grow. Would you like an eclectic collection of exotic classics and? Some organic vegetables are your thing. Or just want an old-fashioned vegetable garden with cooking staples in it? Whatever you pick, you'll find a business that fits your tastes.

Make sure you patronize a reputable seed company for vegetables. If you're unsure where to start, ask a couple of your friends where to buy their seeds. If you know anyone who has a nice garden in the neighborhood, ask them where they get their seeds, or if they have any suggestions. Another way to get tips is by joining a chat group from an online gardener. Gardeners are also happy to support anyone seeking guidance.

Starting a vegetable garden can be an incredibly gratifying experience. Have fun with your vegetable garden but don't forget what we've been discussing. These tips could, later on, they save you time and limit your frustration. Buying your seeds from a trustworthy online company is a simple and cost-effective way to get your garden going.

HOW TO PLANT A FLOWER GARDEN
FOR BEAUTY AND FUNCTION

Many lower gardens are planted solely for their beauty while others may have a more practical purpose. You should put a lot of thought into where your garden should be when you decide you want a flower garden. All of that will depend on the room available to you. You might need to have an "indoor" garden, or a hanging basket or two on your balcony if you stay in a tiny apartment. If you have limited space, the container gardens are nice too. Your green thumb may even satisfy a small herb garden. If you're lucky enough to have a wide enough outdoor area, you'll have more options.

Just as many types of gardens exist, so are many types of flower gardens. It should be borne in mind when preparing yours. Therefore, you should begin with a plan. You could just end up with a mess if you choose some plants and start planting willy nilly.

First, take a quick look at the available space. Draw a quick map of the area, including your home, outbuildings, sources of water, shrubs and trees, and non-digging areas such as underground cables. Draw your plan as close to scale as possible so you don't come across any unexpected surprises like buying too many plants to fit into your available space. On your diagram, you can draw trees as circles.

Now, what do you want out of your garden? Would that be a place to relax? To compensate for a seating room or even for a hammock for napping? Want to get a water feature? Draw those things in your garden design and state where you think they will go. You may want to split it into areas if you have a wide outdoor space — public areas for barbecues and family get-togethers, and more private areas for your own special spot.

How much time will you spend in your garden? Some plants and flowers need substantially more care to keep them safe and beautiful looking. Choose tougher plants if you have limited time that will take less time to tend. Lamps and perennials need more maintenance as they need to be replaced annually. Certainly, some can grow season by season without much work on your part. A large portion of gardening is watching how plants grow in your country's particular environment.

On the front of your house, or along a walkway and drive-way, you might just want to plant a border of flowers. When you have even more time, you might want to have a larger area packed with blooms.

When preparing your garden, remember when each flower will bloom. Spring bulbs, annuals, perennials and flowers bloom in the fall. When you schedule it right, you can have something that blooms all three seasons of the year (or four in some areas).

The more you prepare, the more successful you will be as in any other endeavor. It is easier to just plan a garden "in your head" than to have no plan at all. When you've thought out your strategy, start planting and enjoy the beautiful flowers created by your hard work.

HOW TO GET BEAUTIFUL FLOWERS WITHOUT DAMAGING YOUR BUDGET

Do you wonder how to give your loved ones beautiful flowers and gifts without damaging your budget? Looking for the most cost-effective way to give your friends the gifts? Would you want the scent and freshness of the flowers and an exquisite mix of aesthetically crafted and arranged lovely, elegant flowers to express your good wishes? Today, with improved access and new technology such as the internet and e-commerce, you can send flowers to your friends residing in various corners of the world.

You can give your friends beautiful flowers and bouquets, without hurting your budget. Contact the nearest flower store or floral distributors to start. If they have a larger distribution network and accept online orders, it's even better. You can also pick your gifts over the internet and put your orders online, instead of visiting the stores. They can also provide free and timely delivery of flowers in their service area – including delivery on the same day orders are placed. Digital shopping can be more cost-effective because it avoids middlemen's expenses. Beautifully arranged fresh flower bouquets will cost you, depending on the floral varieties selected, starting from $45. A large range of flowers and colors – rose, ivy, orchid, gerbera, daisy, dahlia, asters – can be selected from the shops. Roses are a favorite of all time; an exquisite heart-shaped bouquet made entirely of prim red roses will cost around $300. The cost of the flowers you have selected could go higher depending on the quality, supply and demand.

Clearly, you have the option to have your own garden, in which selected ornamental plants may grow. You should visit the nearest nursery and select the flowers you wish to include in your gift, learn how to grow them from the nursery and what time of year they will bloom. There are plants bearing flowers in all seasons, some flowering within a season and some flowering for years. Be sure to include other orchid varieties, garden rose, anthurium and some of those decorative leafy plants in your garden. For any occasion, a plastic wrapper with light designs, ribbons and a transparent tape will allow you to make your own gift. You can also buy small size cards/stickers in which you can write your message or heart-shaped bun baskets which will allow you to beautifully arrange the flowers.

Now start saying anything with flowers, at reasonable rates, without damaging your budget.

PROBLEMS GROWING FLOWERS

Even in the best cared for gardens things sometimes go wrong – it is utter nonsense to assume that pests and diseases will only target sickly plants. You must be on against outside invaders, however, nice the beds and borders look, as there are insects and fungal diseases that can destroy your plants and ruin all your efforts. Your plants are likely to be infected by an adversary from inside rather than by an external marauder – these internal causes may be the bad quality of your soil, lack of water, hunger, wind, frost, or you pick the wrong plants or do the wrong things. Before it starts, the golden rule for having healthy flowers is to avoid trouble and deal with it quickly once it is noticed.

Prevent trouble before choosing. If you buy a good stock, it won't be effective in the wrong place. Evite styles would be too delicate for your garden. Don't plant annuals that enjoy the sun or shady areas like under trees – the show is likely to be disappointing.

Have the field fully prepared. A strong-growing plant is more likely than a poor specimen to recover from a plague or disease attack. Waterlogging is one of the worst problems in clayey soils, due to inadequate soil preparation. If you intend to plant perennials, get rid of all weed roots and apply Bromophos to the soil if rodents have gnawed roots elsewhere in the garden.

Plant or sow accordingly. Seed sowing implies doing the right thing at the right time – sowing outdoors too early, and the seeds will rot, plant too late, and the results will be of limited durability. When the seed is sown indoors, note that "hardening" is necessary before the seedlings are moved outdoors.

Never allow garbage to lie about. Boxes, old flowerpots, etc. are a slugs and woodlice breeding site. Rotting plants can be an infectious source and can potentially attract pests to the garden.

Suitable for feeding the plants

Nutrient shortages can lead to many problems – poor growth, undersized blooms, reduced resistance to disease and discolored leaves.

Plants are checked periodically. If treated promptly but can be difficult or impossible to control if left to get out of hand due to ignorance or neglect, act quickly – most pests and diseases can be checked quite easily once you've put a name to the problem.

Deal with trouble as soon as possible by hand removing occasional problems. Minor attacks can often be handled by handpicking a caterpillar or leaf miner out of your garden. If a plant dies unexpectedly, dig it out and closely examine it to find the cause. Examine the roots of soil pests and the ground – take remedial action if the cause is detected.

Keep a small package for pesticides on hand. It will be several days before you can head to the shops, but a sudden greenfly, caterpillar or slugs attack calls for urgent action. So, having a limited number of pesticides in the garden shed for emergency use is a smart idea. For all leaf pests, you will need a bottle of Long-last, a package of General-Purpose Fungicide Mini Slug Pelletsandacarton. Do not buy more than you need – it is easier to purchase a new small container each year instead of carrying packs from one season to the next.

Sprinkle appropriately. When pests or diseases have begun to take hold, swift action will need to be taken. Carefully read the label, and make sure the drug is approved for the plant you want to spray.

Pick a period when the weather is neither sunny nor windy and apply the spray in the evening when the bees have finished working during the flowering season. Using a strong spray, proceed until the leaves are coated and the liquid has just started to run out. Do not aim the spray on to open delicate blooms. Wash out appliances after spraying, then wash your hands then face. Place the packages in a safe position and do not leave the items unlabeled. Not store pesticides or weed killers in a bottle of beer or other tubs.

Recovery to pace with foliar feed. Plants can be invalids, as can humans. The reason may have been a pest or disease attack, and the best way to get things going again is to use a fertilizer that is recommended to spray on the leaves – examples are Instant Bio and Fillip.

The greatest concern with the crop pests is that they are operating unnoticed. Drop Bromophos into the soil before planting, and sprinkle Slug Gard around the stems after planting if you think you have a problem with soil pests or if the site was lawn or rough grassland recently.

Here is a list of some common garden pests and diseases.

ROOT LEATHERJACKET or greyish-brown grubs which can be a serious nuisance on poorly drained soil in herbaceous borders. During a rainy winter, leatherjacket attacks are often worst; they're rarely a nuisance in sandy areas. Sprinkle Slug Gard over the ground if found at the roots of failed plants, and lightly rake in.

MILLEPEDE. Various types exist in the soil, both black and spotted. They appear to curl up when disturbed and should always be killed when found because they damage many plants' underground sections. Areas compromised or diseased are prime targets. Slug Gard can be used to keep control of this plague.

WIREWORM. These rough, glossy insects are a problem in new gardens and in areas adjacent to grassland. They're slow-moving-not like the friendly centipede active. They consume the roots of most flowering plants, and they can burrow up Chrysanthemum stems. Sprinkle Bro-morphos over the surface of the soil where problems arise.

CUTWORM. These are soil-living green, grey or brown caterpillars maybe 2 inches in length. They gnaw both roots and stems, but their tell-tale effect is to cut down on the ground level seedlings and young bedding plants. When this happens, the cutworms near the targeted plants are searched for and killed. Rake in as a preventive in Bromophos.

CHAFER GRUB. These wrinkled white grubs attack the roots of many plants, such as ferns, pot plants and alpines being the worst affected. If a rock plant suddenly dies, search in the soil for the vine weevil's rolled-up grub. If there is one, pick and kill. Using the Hexyl spray push dirt.

Fat-curved grubs feed on the roots of herbaceous border plants throughout the year. There are times when both Chrysanthemums and Dahlias are killed. If you notice these grubs in the dirt, or if you intend to plant them in freshly damaged grassland, sprinkle Bromophos onto the dirt and rake in lightly.

CLUB ROOT. This serious vegetable garden disease which may affect Wallflowers and Stocks. The roots underneath the ground are bloated and twisted, the plants above ground are tiny and die off earlier than usual. The best method is to lime the soil before planting, to prevent Wallflowers from growing year after year on the same site.

CATS are an annual perennial pest. Their scratching disturbs seedbeds and freshly set up bedding plants. The resulting damage to the root will cause seedlings to die. If cats have chosen your flower bed for their toilet, safety is not easy; sprinkle Pepper Dust liberally around the disturbed ground.

BLACK ROOT ROT. A common disease that affects Antir-rhinum, Begonia, Sweet Pea, Geranium, etc. The leaves turn yellow and wilt on the grass. The roots are blackened underground. There is no solution, so avoid the causes — unsterilized indoor compost, un-composted outdoor leaf molds, and replanting the same kind of plant in polluted soil.

An invasion of moles will wreak havoc. The hills thrown up by their tunnels are unsightly and cause significant damage to the surface. Small plants may have their roots dug up. Eradication isn't easy – first try the Mole Smokes. This might be necessary to put in traps or gas them; this work is best performed by a professional exterminator.

How to Grow Tomatoes

If you have a fruit and vegetable garden in mind you certainly want new and juicy tomatoes to grow in it. It's never too late to collect important information as to how tomatoes grow.

The nature of the plant that is put in the garden influences the early harvest and fruit quantity. If you decide to start tomato planting through the use of seeds, then you should give enough time to grow the seedling to allow the first true leaves to sprout before you transplant them. Note that when put in a closed environment, their growth stunts. Tomatoes grow best when they are put for hours in strong direct sunlight or grow in lamps. Placing it in the sunniest part of the garden or a little distance from artificial growing lights is your best choice. Placing them next to trees and buildings isn't advisable.

The wind is favorable for tomatoes; within 5-10 minutes, it is good to position a fan directly at them. Bad drainage of air to the soil causes the physical and root problems. You would have to heat the soil as much as possible by covering the area with black or red plastic two weeks before it is planted. When you test the soil and it can reach a temperature above 60 degrees F, then you are ready to plant tomatoes in the greenhouse.

Good spacing and staking are significant considerations to remember as well. 24-36 inches spacing between plants is best as close spacing can depress the circulation of air as well as cause disease outbreaks. If you intend to grow tomatoes in containers and pots, they need to be buried in greater depth. The roots that grow along the base, will make them grow towards the sun.

Fortunately, the tomatoes grow in any form of soil. You may throw on peat mass, leaf mold, well-rooted manure or compost to enhance the garden. If the soil is prepared, garden fertilizer can be added. For fertilizers the upper 6 inches of soil will work well. The use of ammonia fertilizer is not recommended, so make sure that the soil is warmed before mulching.

Mulching is used to conserve water and to prevent diseases in the soil. If it's mulch earlier, the soil will become shaded and cooled. Mulches are a great help to reduce grazing and weeding by hand. Hay, straw, grass, clippings, paper, or compost are typically used for tomato mulches. Once the plant is 3 inches tall, the leaves which appear an inch above the bottom should be plucked; this is because fungus may grow in leaves which are less likely to get enough sun.

By pinching or pruning, you can remove suckers that develop in two divisions of the crotch joint. The leaves are responsible for producing sugars and for photosynthesis. Be delicate when plant pruning, and do not do so with varieties early-season. Those who are bushy like varieties of late-season or late-season vine, you should take away the side shoots.

Tomatoes need plenty of water so watering should be organized. During the growing process, deep and frequent watering is crucial. Rotting and cracking can result in the inability to water the plant for a week. The plant is more sensitive to its sugar once the ripening starts, so at this point, you can lessen the watering. The tomato plant is susceptible to both man and insect-transmitted diseases. Soil moisture and nutrients may be a battle as well as weeds. Physical problems that aren't caused by insects or illnesses are also present. What you want is the best result for your tomato plant. Going through those tips will lead you in the right direction.

Tomatoes are best grown indoors and only brought outdoors.

Whether your tomato plants are bigger, you'll need a tray or several small plant containers, some compost built to grow tomatoes, and some larger containers. As they love warmth and sunshine, I always start my tomato off indoors; they usually do well in a windowsill.

Fill a pot with compost and then position the seeds on top of the compost and put a fine layer of compost on top of the seeds and pat it down. Water well and position it in a window sill. I generally do this around April time, although it can be done sooner when planting inside and slightly later than this both inside and in a greenhouse.

Make sure your plant pots or trays are still well numbered, so you know what you've planted. If the plants are large enough to remove, they can be put again in larger pots that contain a decent tomato compost, once they are at least 5 inches in height, a decent liquid tomato food can be provided once a week while watering. The plants may be moved outdoors in their pots during sunny or warm days when the plants are well developed but brought in at night when it gets colder.

When the weather is warm enough day and night, they can permanently be left outside.

Use the sticks to sustain their growth once your plants have reached a considerable height. Always make sure that your tomato plants are well watered for complete and juicy tomatoes and particularly when tomato growth is found.

HOW TO MANAGE GROWING TOMATOES

When you have a vegetable garden, you're possibly going to add tomatoes as one of the plants. While tomatoes are indeed fruits, they seem to be treated by everyone as vegetables.

Tomato plants are broken down into two distinct types. The first type forms a flower which stops the plant from growing at the top of the plant. The second form, called indeterminate, is becoming much taller. This may pose a problem in colder climates because, before cooler weather arrives, the tomatoes will not be ready for harvest. I like soil and really warm air too. So, if they aren't protected, they will die in colder weather.

To help protect the tomato plants, small greenhouse-like structures may be used to cover them. Earlier in the growing season, maybe by planting seedlings indoors or in a greenhouse, longer growing plants should be started where possible.

Growing tomatoes can also pose problems in warmer climates. They can be planted in full light but may become sunburned. The answer here is obvious: a partly sunny vine.

Tomatoes are also vulnerable to rodents and other illnesses.

Blossom end rot is a soft brown spot at the tomato rim. This is caused by a lack of calcium. This disease may be due to incorrect watering procedures as water carries calcium from the soil to the tomato plant root.

Try to take the infected tomatoes off the plant to offer a chance to grow other, better, tomatoes.

Of course, to avoid this problem, it is best to water correctly in the first place. Water enough so that the roots grow stronger. Mulch around the plants also to protect them from drying out. For good tomatoes, the pH level of the soil should be around 6.5.

Tomato hornworms and aphids are the plagues that can damage your tomato crop.

Tomato hornworms are larvae of 4 inches that are hard to see because they are the same green color as the tomato plant. Look down their sides for the long white lines, and a black dot on the back. You'll need to watch for them and pick them off as soon as possible.

These hornworm larvae are transformed into large brown moths that can grow to have a 5-inch wingspan. Planting marigold and basil plants around the base of the tomato plants will prevent the eggs from being laid on them by the adult moths.

Aphids can cause growing tomatoes problems, too. Such little bugs are just around 1/10-inch long and they can be hard to find. You could try washing them off with a garden hose. Unfortunately, they're going to keep coming here.

You can try planting petunias or anise around the plants but some insecticide soaps will remove the bugs without hurting the tomato plants or the people who eat the tomatoes.

It may sound like growing tomatoes is a lot of trouble, but it really isn't. It's well worth the work put into getting good tomatoes to eat. Feed them properly and watch for rodents and diseases. You can then be confident of a successful tomato harvest to eat.

HOW TO GROW LETTUCE

Want to grow your own lettuce but have no outdoor space? No trouble. Lettuce is just one of those vegetables you can grow indoors with easiness. In fact, growing vegetables indoors for your own consumption is the most economical way to make sure you eat high-quality produce even if you don't have plenty of space around.

Lettuce is one of those vegetables that are nowadays commonly grown by individual farmers. This is almost so because lettuce is one of the healthiest vegetables. This is filled with a good portion of antioxidants and vitamins. Plus, for anyone who loves to prepare and eat salads, it is very much a staple.

However, much growing and harvesting lettuce is simple, there are still a few things you need to keep in mind during the preparation process before the lettuce is harvested. Here are some of the following:

PREPARATION: if you're going to grow lettuce indoors, you'd have to prepare the containers or grow boxes where you'll be sowing the seeds. In this end, a good container are those clamshell boxes used by the supermarket in displaying lettuce and other fresh fruit and vegetables. You can, of course, use other boxes just as long as it has at least 10 inches of width. To allow water flow, you'd need to make a few gashes on the bottom portion of the package.

You need to prepare the soil you will be using after you have received the package. You will need to use good soil to achieve high-quality produce. Hummus or potting soil, peat, perlite, and vermiculite will be a fine combination. Place in your jar an equal mix of those.

SOWING: the seeds can be planted 1/8 of an inch deep when all is already prepared. Before that, you need to gently cover it with the soil mix and lightly spray it with water.

Germination will occur within about one to two weeks of planting. You will then thin out the seedlings to make way for the growing lettuce. I strongly recommend you take the smaller ones out to allow the stronger seedlings some room to grow. You can also transplant those into other containers if you prefer.

CARE: it is recommended that fertilizers rich in nitrogen, potassium and phosphorus be added every two weeks. In addition, you do need to frequently water the lettuce to keep the soil moist but don't overdo it to make it muddy.

Sunlight is also one of the things that the lettuce very much requires. To produce lush and high-quality lettuce, you must keep the developing lettuce exposed to light for at least 10 hrs. Nevertheless, you do need to make sure the temperature does not rise too high. For proper growth lettuce requires a cool climate.

Selecting vegetables that can be grown in containers can be your best choice when you want to grow your vegetables but do not have too much room for them. In this case, one of the best ways to do that is to learn how to grow lettuce. Lettuce is not a lot of trouble growing and can even be grown in containers.

Apart from this, lettuce has a very exceptional nutritional value which makes it one of the most popular vegetables produced by organic home growers. This is high in vitamins A, K, C, antioxidants and beta-carotene. Also, if you're fond of salad, there's no way to prepare your salad better and fresher than using the produce from your own little garden.

Growing lettuce might not be a lot of trouble, but there are many things you need to have in mind to make sure you grow high-quality harvest lettuce. Several of these things are:

Containers Preparation

First things first – you need to find the best containers you can use for your own little greenhouse. You may use window boxes, planters, or even the container used for showing lettuce or other fruits or vegetables in most supermarkets. Once you've found a suitable container, you need to make some gashes on the bottom to allow water to flow when the plants are watered.

The next step will be to prepare the soil within the containers that you are to put. For this, the best form of soil will be humus soil. You may also add a section equal to perlite and vermiculite. Both can help to properly absorb air and water, thereby allowing your plants to grow optimally.

Planting the seeds

You can start sowing the lettuce seeds once the containers are ready. Make sure you are using high-quality seeds from reputable brands. The seeds should be sown 1/4 of an inch deep. Gently sprinkle with water after sowing.

The seeds are to germinate for about one or two weeks. You can thin out the lettuce after seeing growth leaving extra room for the lusher ones. You have the right to transplant seedlings that you took out of the containers.

Care and maintenance

You can expect to pick fresh lettuce from your own little garden at any time of the year with due care. Just make sure it meets the conditions the plants need. For example, the lettuce must be regularly watered. Yet it has to be the way that only keeps the soil moist.

Another thing is that lettuce would need light exposure, too. In reality, it can allow light exposure for 10-12 hours. However, you have to know that lettuce grows best in cooler conditions while exposing it to the sunlight. That is why you must always make sure that the temperature is not too hot.

HOW TO GROW BROCCOLI SPROUTS

Perhaps one of the easiest vegetables to grow is practical steps for you to pursue are broccoli sprouts. Learning how to grow broccoli sprouts wouldn't take much experience in gardening. Also, to enjoy new broccoli sprouts you wouldn't have to wait for seasons either. You'll be able to grow broccoli sprouts fresh from your own garden in as little as a week.

It's almost a common knowledge that broccoli is nutrient-filled. It contains a large amount of vitamins A, B, C, E and K as well as other nutrients known to combat cancer, such as protein, calcium, zinc and antioxidants. That is probably why broccoli sprouts would be placed anyone's list of vegetables to be grown indoors.

Broccoli sprouts, apart from these health benefits, are also considered to be more forgiving than most other vegetables. Thus, growing your own broccoli sprouts wouldn't be that much of a hassle.

So, here are the practical steps in growing your own broccoli sprouts to get you started:

1. First of all, you need to have packed everything you may need. The stuff you will need are broccoli seeds labeled for sprouting, shallow pots, soil potting and plastic wrapping. You will also want to get all of your basic garden tools ready in case you need them.

2. Soak the seeds at room temperature the night before. When choosing seeds, make sure you pick the correct seeds by carefully inspecting the mark. It should be labeled to sprout.

In addition, I strongly recommend using organic seeds. To make them last longer, some commercial seeds are treated with special chemicals but growing full-grown broccoli doesn't pose too much of a problem. When you grow sprouts, the chemical tends to be more concentrated.

3. Get ready for the bin. Only fill it up with the right amount of potting soil.

4. Scatter the seeds on the field. You don't have to think about getting too much seed or spacing when sprinkled. You are not going to grow full-grown broccoli, so space isn't going to be an issue here. Then, again cover it with another thin layer of potting soil.

5. Place plastic wrap over the pot. Bore some holes into the plastic wrap to allow the circulation of some air.

6. Store them in a dry, warm place.

Be sure that it is located away from the sun's intense heat. You'll be able to see the sprouts after two days. The sprout shall be fit for harvest by the end of 5 days.

Broccoli is a cool-seasonal crop that can be grown in spring as well as in fall. The plants grow in cool climates and should be planted in hot summer areas under shade. Broccoli grows best in warm, moist soil with a slightly acidic pH between 6.0 and 7.0 and between 15.5 and 18 ° C (60–65 ° F) at temperatures. Broccoli has a high demand for nitrogen, and due to the decreased soil microbial activity during winter and late fall, organic matter should be applied to the soil during the year to ensure sufficient nutrient supply when broccoli is planted. Additionally, broccoli needs daily water to prevent the plants from seeding, particularly during drought. Plant broccoli to ensure optimum head size is achieved. Broccoli seeds can be planted directly or be started indoors for transplantation. Spring plantings should be completed in your region 2–3 weeks before the last frost date, and fall plantings should be done about 100 days before the first fall frost. Plant seed 1.3 cm (0.5 in.) deep in small groups of 2–3 seeds and around one week after emergence, thin to a final spacing of 30–60 cm (12–24 in) within the row, making 90 cm (36 in) between rows. After planting, keep soil uniformly moist. When beginning indoors, plant seeds in peat pots to reduce damage to the roots during transplantation. The seedling can be planted outdoors at the same time as seeds are planted using the spacing mentioned above when they are 3–4 weeks old. Plant transplants in the field slightly deeper than they are in their container. Keep the soil moist to ensure good fertility. Broccoli has a very shallow root system for general care and maintenance and should be avoided cultivating the soil around the plants to eliminate weeds. Provide adequate and even moisture to plants (about two in a week) to keep plants fertile and prevent them from bolting and to avoid wetting the heads of the flower as they grow. Mulching around the plants helps maintain soil moisture and reduces soil temperature. Broccoli is ready to be harvested when the buds

in the flower are firm and tightly packed together. Harvest
before the buds open by cutting the stalk of the head below
the head at an angle of 45 °, around 13–20 cm (5–8 in).
After first harvest, side-shoots will continue to produce.

HOW TO GROW APPLE TREES FROM A SEED

I't's a long-term investment that you need to grow apples first. Apples growing requires a considerable amount of time and effort. Also, if an apple tree in your backyard is one of your fondest childhood memories, harvesting your own apples is a rewarding aspect of gardening.

Site Selection

Make sure that you have space for at least two trees before you start growing apples. Usually two apple trees bear enough fruit to have a sufficient supply for a family of four. Apple trees need to thrive in full sun, meaning they need at least six hours of sunlight every day. Also, dwarf forms should be spaced at least eight feet apart. It's also important to ensure good drainage for your trees. While apple trees tolerate a variety of soil types, sandy loam is preferred to sandy clay loam with a pH of around 6.5.

Choosing cultivars

You probably wonder why you need to grow two trees. The apple trees are incompatible with one another. In other words, the most industrious bee (bees are the primary pollinators of apple trees) cannot get two trees of the same type to bring forth fruit. So, you typically need two trees of different varieties to grow apples. Some nurseries sell apple trees which have two or more compatible cultivars grafted on the same tree; to be on the safe side (and for a family of four to get enough apples), you do need two trees. a flowering crab can pollinate your fruit-bearing apple tree and is useful in pest deterrence.

While apple trees grow from seed, the development of an apple harvest from seed takes several years and a significant amount of nurturing. Buying either bare-root or container-grown trees from your favorite garden nursery is the best way to start growing apples.

In addition to the fruit size, taste, and color, your nursery professional will recommend cold-hardy trees for your area, bloom at about the same time as compatible with pollination, and are resistant to disease. You will find that buying disease-resistant cultivars gives your apple tree a generous reduction in maintenance time!

Such distinctions between cultivars need to be made when choosing trees from a catalog or website. Look for catalogs and places that list cultivars that are compatible with you.

How high the tree grows depends on the type of tree you are planting too. Dwarf varieties reach 8 to 10 feet in height, semi-dwarf trees grow 10 to 15 feet in height and standard trees growing reach 20 feet or more in height.

While their yield is smaller, the dwarf and semi-dwarf root-stock usually bear fruit of the same size as standard size trees and are easier to handle overall.

This Is How It's Done Next

The apple seeds must be carefully removed from the apple without destroying it. The new apples preferably selected locally.

Let this dry for a few days at room temperature. Take a plastic tub to the bottom and apply a wet paper towel.

Within the container place 15 to 20 apple seeds. Use another damp paper towel to cover the apple seeds and cool the jar.

After 2 to 3 weeks, the roots sprout from your apple seeds. Remember that it will sprout about 30 percent of the seeds. Paper towel must still be moist so your plastic tub must be sealed with a lid.

Plant it into a container filled with black earth for each sprouting seed. Let it grow to a minimum height of 2 feet before planting in your yard.

So, you have now grown an apple tree from a simple seed. The final step is to grease your apple tree, so it grows the right sort of apples like Macintosh, Courtland or others.

Propagation

Apple trees grow best in the tropics, so they allow a mild growing season and a cold winter at higher latitudes to break their dormancy. The tree will bloom at these latitudes in spring, and fruit will grow in fall. Throughout the tropics, the leaves will stay on the tree longer so that it becomes basically evergreen and bending shoots to build a large tree will occur sporadically during the year unless the tree becomes able to implement a consistent period throughout the forest. The traditional method of apple propagation is by budding. It is strongly recommended, when planting an apple nursery or orchard, to plant seedlings budded from rootstock to avoid an increase in bud dormancy. In the first year, budded trees should be pruned to promote new growth of the shoots. Apple trees in the tropics need careful management to make the heavy crop loads sustainable. This involves bending leaves, pruning tips and defoliating trees as well. Flowers are also removed, usually after two years, to encourage growth before first fruit production. Apple trees may also be propagated by grafting and layering of the mounds. Grafting includes combining the lower part (rootstock) of one plant with the upper part (scion) of another. Grafting is typically performed during the dormant season, and the dormant scion and stock wood must be used. Mound layering is used for the propagation of clonal rootstocks in apples. Soil is mounted around shoots that have been cut back, thus stimulating the roots at the base of the shoots to expand. A year before propagation starts, the stock plants are planted in rows with a diameter of 8–10 mm (0.3–0.4 in) and then cut back to 45–60 cm (17.7–23.6 in.) They are then managed for a year. The plants are cut back again in the spring, this time to 2.5 cm (1 in.) above ground. Gradually, new shoots grow, and more soil and bark are added to the mounds around the plants. May continue this cycle through the growing season. The shoots are then harvested by cutting near to the bases. The mother stool beds are then left exposed until the new shoots have expanded further, and another process of hilling begins.

HOW TO GROW ARTICHOKES

Do you wonder how artichokes grow?

While not everyone is fond of eating this wonderful food, it is a vegetable worth growing for those of us who do it. You know how good this vegetable can be if you're one of the lucky ones who loves them.

The section of the artichoke we eat is the artichoke plant's undeveloped flower bud. The best part of everything is called the nucleus of an artichoke.

Globe artichokes are the most prevalent form of artichokes people consume. Seeds to globe artichokes can be found in seed catalogues. Artichoke seedlings can be purchased at your nearest nursery. Only call ahead and inquire when it will deliver their artichokes shipments.

Find a sunny spot with well-drained soil in your yard. Prepare the soil by digging into it approximately one foot deep and mixing compost with chicken or rabbit manure.

If your winters are mild and you don't hit temperatures below 15 degrees, then you can directly sow your artichoke seeds into the forest. Plant your artichoke seeds 1/4" into the soil. If you need to start your artichoke seedlings indoors, do so eight weeks before the last frost. Allow plenty of space. Plant your seeds 3 feet apart. Artichoke plants can grow up to 3'-4' high and 6' wide. When the artichoke plants are being planted into the soil, place the artichokes so that the crown is just above the ground. If you've got the crown of your plant above ground, whether you're starting from seed or not, mulch around the base to maintain the soil. Keep watering your garden. Your soil should be damp, but not soggy, or full of water. Upon planting, you should mix sand into heavy soil, to help the soil drain well. Or, to allow proper drainage, you can plant your artichokes on mounds. Your artichoke plant fertilizes daily. Until the bud begins to open, pick your artichoke and when the plant is still green and thick. It will mean that you have the best, most savory plant to eat. Be patient; first-year artichokes cannot deliver. Continue to look properly for your plant and you'll soon be reaping the rewards. Although the majority of artichokes are grown in California, they can be grown in other parts of the country if given the proper care. Simply follow the "how to grow artichokes" tips above, and you should enjoy wonderful results.

Have fun in the garden! Three totally distinct genera are known as artichokes. The Cynara scolymus, the globe artichoke, useful both as a table delicacy and an ornamental border plant, then the Helianthus tuberosus, the Jerusalem artichoke, a homely and nutritious vegetable, and lastly the Stachys Sieboldi, the Chinese artichoke, bearing edible tubers, but of small consequence. The globe artichoke is a strong fleshy-rooted hardy perennial producing large handsome foliage and great thistle-like heads, the scales of which are the edible portion. It requires a deeply dug rich soil in an open, sunny position. The plants require a square yard of space each. They need an abundance of water and liquid manure in summer, and the crowns should be covered with loose litter during severe frosts. Flower-heads are cut for use just before they open. The plant might be used as an ornamental border flower, the open blossoms being bright rosy - heliotrope borne on stems from 3 feet to 6 feet high.

There is no great difficulty in growing the artichoke from Jerusalem because it prefers a free soil, will repay generous treatment with abundant crops but will yield good yield even on bad soil. The planting distance should be 1 foot between sets, 3 feet between rows, at a depth of 6 inches No unearthing needed, and if left in the ground until necessary for use, the tubers are uninjured by frost.

In the case of Jerusalem artichokes, the simple method of selecting the appropriate number of sound tubers to be planted out as mentioned above affects an increase in stock. Globe artichokes are combined with offsets that sprout from the sides of fully formed crowns. During April, remove these from the ground. They are best plotted in gritty compost and plunged into a frame to the rims of the pots. Keep close until signs of growth indicate that ventilation is required. Gradually harden and plant out where you are to live throughout the season.

Truly good to eat, the globe artichoke is unfortunately not a favorite in the typical home garden. But, if you have the room to support a fair number of plants, then it's certainly worth trying.

In reality, even if you don't have tons of space, they're such attractive plants, just for fun, you might grow one row as a frontier.

Globe artichokes are a type of thistle possibly originating in southern Europe and the Mediterranean region, covering not only Europe but also the top of Africa, north of the Sahara Desert.

The plant itself is a very pretty green-grey leafy perennial; its fruit is the "globe." The heart is the most important part of the fruit but the leaves on the head are scrumptious as well. You may also consume the stem of young plants around 15 cm, or 6 inches. Only the hairy choke must be removed in the middle of the fruit (or globe).

There are lots of artichokes cooking recipes, some of which concentrate on different sauces that you dip the artichoke leaves into. There are also recipes that focus on stuffing and then baking the globe or using other vegetables to bake the hearts. But the best way to cook them is to cut the hard outer leaves (not all the leaves) and then boil the entire artichoke fruit until the end of the stem is tender. Strain and pour on a little melted butter (better still garlic butter) and sprinkle with salt and pepper. Then all you do is cut each leaf with your teeth and scrape out the tender part at the bottom. Discard every remotely tough part. At the bottom of the leaves, you will find the heart nestling, at the very top of the plant. Break it in half, and then remove the choke before eating.

Whereas globe artichokes will continue to expand for about four years. In terms of space they occupy in a veggie field, they are infamous for their low yield. If you DO have land, you do need sunshine, well-maintained soil, and a well-drained location. The maximum pH would be 6.5, a very slightly acidic pH.

Artichokes are much easier and quicker to raise from seedlings (as opposed to seeds) or from the rooted suckers of existing seedlings instead of older ones. When you grow from seed, it will take five to six months to transplant, until they are large enough.

When they have developed your artichokes, they won't need much care. At the base of the stem, you'll need to cut weeds and dead leaves (not to be confused with fruit leaves). Mulching, including side dressing with garden fertilizer or chicken manure, is also helpful.

The artichoke stem will branch out on top of each and form a flower. Enable the bud to grow and develop, but harvest before it opens, and make flowers.

Flower gardening, herb gardening, and vegetable gardening can all be a rewarding experience. They are an addition to any garden or even a house. Taking an idea and transforming it into an actual garden of your dreams can often be a little daunting, if not planned properly. No matter what sort of garden you're speaking about, they all owned specific features and purposes there.

Gardens can be built for a number of purposes, indoor decoration, an enhancement to your landscape, in window boxes to add value to the look of your house, containers or pots to spice up a porch or patio or just a garden to provide you with cut flowers or vegetables. These can all be equally satisfying and can be achieved using ecological processes.

The pleasure of preparing a garden or gardens, seeing a plant grow from seed and blossom into a piece of natural art, working the soil and realizing the natural benefits that it can give you are all about organic gardeners. They love nature, study techniques and work with it, not against it, and get the best out of it.

Step one is planning your organic garden is to learn how plant life grows naturally within your field. Watch nature, study and follow its instructions, it has many advantages of having a healthy garden which can provide you with. Grow green and get the reward nature will naturally offer you in your gardening practices.

An environmentally friendly and sustainable way of gardening.

Organic Cultivation is in harmony with nature and away from cultivation. To grow a healthy and profitable crop in a way that is safer for you as well as for the environment.

HOW TO GROW ASPARAGUS

Asparagus is a perennial plant with edible stems, erect and tiny branches with even tinier flowers that develop into red berries with black asparagus seeds. Former botanists in the Liliaceae family noticed that Asparagus is alone in a community and repositioned the 120 species in the Asparagaceae genus. It is a high-end gourmet food item but if you know how to grow asparagus then it is an easy way to add a delicate flavor to your meals.

Understanding how to grow asparagus dates back to when it was first cultivated in Greece, 2500 years ago. Indeed, asparagus is for stalk or shooting from the Greek term. The asparagus was praised for its medicinal properties long before it was used as a food item. Multiple reasons for growing asparagus. Once an asparagus bed has been set up, asparagus is the first vegetable that is ready for the table in the springtime and would supply your family with a fresh and firm vegetable treat for close to 20 years, each crown in your bed growing up to 1/2 pound of spears per year. While supermarkets stock both canned and frozen asparagus, none of them compare the unique flavor of freshly harvested and picked asparagus that you get.

As asparagus plants grow, they develop a mat that spreads horizontally rather than vertically with long, tubular roots. The one-year-old root system is called the crown of asparagus. While asparagus can be started from seed, it is most frequently started from transplanting crowns bought from a reputable crown grower. Those who want to know how to grow asparagus must have an abundance of patience, as it takes three years to establish an asparagus bed from crowns. Asparagus ferns emerge from the second year of growth with a few spindly spears. While your bed will grow thicker and more durable spears in the third year, they shouldn't be harvested for more than a month to allow roots and crowns to develop themselves further.

Plant asparagus crowns one to two feet wide in a trench. Place the crowns as deep as 6 inches and separate as 9 to 12 inches. Asparagus quickly grows in any well-drained soil. The delicate asparagus ferns were called "sparrow grass," and were found growing wild on English rivers. Asparagus permitted to stand in water, however, develops root rot which can easily kill a complete bed. The roots of asparagus continue to "grow," as the bed matures. Usually gardeners apply soil to the rows of a mature asparagus bed to hold the crowns underground. Asparagus is also vulnerable to frost in the late spring, which kills spears that emerge. Take care to keep your bed filled with asparagus until the danger of frost is gone.

Asparagus is considered to be a hardy perennial type of vegetable plant that produces fleshy, tender, green "spears" or stems with caps that form buds. This will feature feathery, fern-like foliage when grown to maturity. Many homeowners want to know how to grow asparagus so they will spend a very long time in the garden-from about 15 years or so.

If you are planting 30 to 40 asparagus plants when it comes to yield, it can already feed about 2 to 4 people on many course meals. Asparagus crowns are best planted during the spring season.

HOW TO GROW ASPARAGUS

Phase 1 – Prepare the seeds approximately 12 to 14 weeks before the final frost. This is because Asparagus requires three years before it is completely productive and developed. Actually, sow the seeds in flats 1 1/2 inch thick. Grow up the seedlings until they reach age one.

Phase 2 –Find a place for the crowns of your asparagus. This should be in full sunshine, but partial shade can also be tolerated. This also requires well-drained soil, no more than 6.0 pH.

Phase 3 – Loosen the soil. Make sure it has a range of 8 to 10. Add compost which is well-age. Pick the one-year-old crowns which are well-rooted and not dry as asparagus is grown from crowns.

Phase 4 – Dig a furrow or trench about 10 cm wide and 10 -12 cm deep.

Phase 5 – Position around the bottom of the trench around 2-4-inch tall mounds of loose soil. Set the crown spacing in the trenches to about 18 to 28 inches apart. Next, distribute the crowns uniformly around the bottom of the trench before covering it with two inches more of soil.

Phase 6 – Apply some high fertilizer of nitrogen (5-10-19) before the spears emerge in the spring, and another at the end of the harvest.

Phase 7 – When the spears begin to develop in spring, slowly fill the trench up to the top. The air should be moist but not hot.

Stuff to remember:

-the beds with asparagus should be well weeded.

-Asparagus plants need a cold dormancy time.

For Asparagus plants, root vegetables are not suitable companions. Parsley, basil, and onions are healthy ones.

Asparagus harvesting can be done when they are already three years old or when fully grown. You need to cut the spears down slightly below ground level in the third season. When doing so, make sure the spears that have not yet emerged are not harmed. If the spears are 8-10 inches long, cut them down to at least a pencil diameter. The best harvest periods are for two weeks on the third year, and then plants for four weeks or up in the fourth year.

When the buds start feathering out, you can no longer eat them.

HOW TO GROW GRAPES

It seems impossible to find someone who doesn't know what the grapes are like. They are grown all around the world and the majority of people love them. In the botanical sense, these morsels of juicy delicacy are berries. They produce at least six individual fruits in bunches. Some varieties grow bunches that numbers an incredible 300 grapes!

Grapes can be grown to eat or to make wine. Table grapes are the ones to eat, and wine grapes are used to produce wine. Centuries of cultivation and research have led to the production of grapes only of a specific branch of plant science. This particular science is called viticulture, and it deals with everything the grapes. Breeds and varieties, soil structure and access to the light, practically all that has to do with how to grow grapes, comes under the viticultural umbrella.

You need to learn what you want to do with the grapes before you ask yourself how to grow grapes. Would this be to make wine, or to eat? Then follow the same step-by-step planting procedures but the precise specifications can vary depending on what you expect to grow.

Table grapes require good drainage and fertile soil. It means that there must not be too high a proportion of clay to loam or sand. So much clay allows a lot of water to stay in the soil, which will cause the roots of the grapevine to rot. The amount of sunlight obtained by the plant is important for the production of fruit sugars.

Start planning your farm or land plot. A lot of sunlight should be provided at the location. To allow for growth, the plants should be about 6 feet apart. Check your ground. Is that relatively fertile? Is it draining well? If not, then apply compost and loosen before planting. It is time to start constructing a trellis after this for the vine to cling to. It just should be tall enough to make it easier to choose. Make sure you pick the wood that doesn't easily rot under the elements.

We can only start the actual planting now. Dig out plant holes. The holes will be wider than the vineyards you intend to plant. It is because when you place it back over the roots, you want the soil to become loose. Using string to bind the strongest tendril to your trellis, not wire that can cause harm to the vine. Water the plants without the rain being enough for them to keep them alive. The weakest or unhealthiest vines should be pruned during the dormant season. It will improve the fruit price.

When the vine starts to bear fruit, the time has come to prepare for harvest. The grapes are selected at the right time to ensure optimum sweetness and juiciness. A hydrometer can prove to be useful in determining your grape sugar content and telling you when to start harvesting.

Wine grapes are more difficult to obtain. Each grape variety produces specific qualities in wine and will also have different growing demands. The steps for growing grapes are the same, no matter how. Plan your garden, build your trellises and cultivate your vineyards. Specific techniques are used to facilitate the production of different grape qualities that will influence the wine.

If you are serious about growing wine grapes, it's best to ask a winemaker. They will tell you the different varieties and specifications, and how to grow grapes for winemaking. Note, with all that said, that the grapes need time. You will need to be careful in setting up and taking care of your plants, but each second and every drop of sweat will be worth the end result.

PROPAGATION REQUIREMENTS

When attempting to grow grape, first consideration is to pick different based on the prevailing local climate, with the best production occurs in hot, dry areas. American varieties tend to like the cold, while European hybrids do better in hotter, drier regions. In general, vines should be grown in full in well-drained soil and at a place where sufficient circulation air is available to reduce the occurrence of disease. While choosing a planting site, low lying areas should be avoided as this can lead to water accumulation during periods of rainy weather Vines prefer a soil with a little acidic to neutralize pH between 6.0 and 7.0 and require a trellis system to aid the weight of the fruit in the vines. Grapevines are typically planted in Spring as dormant bare root vines. Young plants for planting in the home garden can be purchased from nurseries and garden centers. Grapevines need a trellis, which should be built before the vines are planted in the soil. The trellis helps to sustain the fruit's weight and protects the vines from damage, while also increasing air circulation and reducing canopy disease. You will also find a more decorative form, such as an arbor, to support the vines. Fresh plants will be planted out in spring after all frost is gone. Dig a hole approximately 30 cm (12 in) deep and 30 cm (12 in) long for each plant, spaced 1.8–3.0 m (6–10 ft) apart, and plant the vine at the same level as the nursery. It is essential that the graft union is not covered in soil. Tamp the soil around the plants and apply any soil left over. To have just two or three fresh buds, the freshly planted vines should be cut back, and watered lightly. Training In order to establish good root systems for grapevines and to sustain heavy fruit loads, new vines should not be permitted to grow fruit for the first two to three years after planting. The vine is to produce new shoots, some of which should be allowed to expand while the others are cut back. This allows the vine to fill with leaves providing energy for an extensive root system. The latest shoots are to be mounted to the trellis. Choose two to three of the strongest canes on each plant at the start of the second year of production and cut back the rest. Enable three or four shoots on each cane to grow and add to the trellis. Eliminate any forming flower clusters. Pruning is an important component of healthy grape production and should be performed annually in early Spring while the vines remain dormant and before the buds start swelling. Most of the growth of the previous years will be removed from the third year on. The more buds left on each plant, the more fruit it grows, but caution must be taken to ensure that too many are not left, as the resulting fruit will not ripen. Throughout the growing season, fruit clusters can be removed as needed.

HOW TO GROW BLACKBERRIES

Blackberries aren't just yummy; they're easy to grow too. Most people choose to grow these crops on their backyards for this very purpose alone. If you're one of those so keen on learning how to grow blackberries right in your backyard, it's an easy step-by-step method that you can handle easily.

It is important to know what makes this fine fruit special, before planting blackberries. Blackberries are known for being highly nutritious. These are high in vitamin C, calcium and vitamin E. They also have phytonutrients that help combat aging and some cancers. These do have an abundance of soluble fiber that helps to reduce cholesterol. Not only this, but they also contain tannins that are protective in the preservation of taut tissues and in the prevention of bleeding. Last, but not least, they have phytoestrogens that can shield women from breast cancer and cervical cancer.

There are essentially two types of blackberries – the trailing, and the erect varieties. We distinguish by the growth patterns of their canes. Erect blackberries feature rigid, arching, self-supporting canes. They are more immune to cold. They have canes that aren't self-helping for trailing blackberries. They're also called dewberries in the East. So long as you leave the canes the ground and then mulch them during the winter season, they can flourish in colder areas.

What you need to know is where to grow blackberries. For your garden, you will choose a sunny area with good air circulation, water drainage and a pH of about 6.0 to 7.0.

You'll need to keep the roots moist before planting. You will have to work in the soil with plenty of organic matter and then mulch to keep out the weeds. Begin planting as soon as the soil warms up.

Build a hole that is deep enough, which does not bend the roots. Trim the canes to promote new growth. Make sure the plants are set inside rows that are 7 feet apart, about 2 feet apart. Trellising is critical for cane support.

Remember that summer-bearing berries over second-year canes will grow fruit. You need to prune spent canes on the ground level during the fall of the second year, and then thin the others to around four canes for each foot of the path. You must also cut off those suckers that grow beyond the line. The remaining blackberry canes are then cut to 7 cm.

Tips on How to Plant Blackberries

These seeds require stratification when it comes to propagation and sowing. They're best sown in a cold frame during early autumn. They require the stratification of a month at about 3 degrees C for stored seeds, so they are best sown the earliest possible time of the year. You will need to select the seedlings in cold frames once they are big enough to handle and grow on. So, during the final part of spring the next year, plant them out in their permanent positions.

The blackberries prefer medium to dark soils such as sandy, loamy and clay soils when it comes to soil conditions. Both need to be well-drained, but in poor soils they often develop cay. They do prefer basic, neutral and acid soils, but can grow in very alkaline and very acidic soils as well. It also requires moist soil and can withstand the conditions of drought as well.

Blackberries can also grow in full-shade, semi-shade or in no shade at all.

Propagation and specific requirements

Blackberries grow best in temperate regions with hot summers and gentle winters, as they are resistant to cold weather. They grow best when the daytime temperatures are about 25 ° C (77 ° F). Blackberries choose full sun (minimum six hours of direct sunlight) and must be planted in well-drained soil, high in organic matter, and 6–6.5 pH. Drainage in blackberry propagation is important since the plants are vulnerable to root rot. Blackberries should not be sow in low lying areas where water can build up, so there is a need for a post-support system or trellis to support the fruit weight on plants. During their second year of growth, blackberry canes are biennial and bear berries. The canes are referred to as primocanes in their first year of growth and the ones in the second year of growth are referred to as fruiting canes or floricanes. The young canes are green in color, while the older floricanes are tougher and have a woody coating that makes it easy to tell apart. Preparation Soil can need to be prepared up to two years before planting if significant modifications are needed. Acidic soil can be altered with lime to raise the pH to a level suitable for blackberries. Planting a cover crop or adding manure or compost will increase the organic content. Avoid planting blackberries where previously grown peppers, eggplant, tomatoes or potatoes as these plants are host to Verticillium fungi that can cause root rot in blackberries. Choose a variety that fits your place. Planting and trellising Most blackberry varieties are very robust and the use of a support system such as a trellis can help protect the canes against wind damage while still supporting the fruit crop weight. Before or at planting, the trellis should be built to avoid damage to the young plants once they are in the field. A post and wire device is the standard way of backing red blackberry canes. This approach involves running two wires which are about 60 cm (2 ft) apart vertically between staked wooden posts in the ground. The lower wire should be located 90 cm (3 ft) from the ground and from the ground at the upper 1.5 m

(5 ft). They can then tie the blackberry canes to the wires. A second alternative is a post- and wire-like T-trellis, except the vertical wooden posts each have two crossbars to connect the cable. Two pairs of wires run in parallel, one above the other. For the lower wire located 90 cm (3 ft) from the ground also the upper 1,5 m (5 ft) the ground, the vertical posts will be spaced 3.6–4.6 m (12-15 ft.) apart. Blackberry plants are typically grown from bare-root plants or tissue-cultured plants in the home garden. It should be planted in early Spring when the danger of any serious frost has passed. Usually, the plants are planted in a row, and the suckers fill in the spaces to create a hedge. Plant 70 cm (27.5 in) apart, allowing for 2.4–3 m (8–10 ft) between rows. Pruning makes the plants to fill in the row during the growing season to a width of about 30–38 cm (12–15 in); Remove from this row any suckers that are made. Cut the fruity canes of summer-fruiting varieties down to ground level after harvest. Select 6–8 of each plant's strongest young canes and tie them to support wires so they are spaced 8–10 cm (3–4 in.) apart. Cut all autumn fruiting varieties canes down to ground level after harvest. If necessary, to prevent crowding, cut back canes in the summer as needed.

GROWING, PLANTING AND PROPAGATING

GREEN BEANS

To plan a bean garden properly, understanding the whole process of growth of bean plants will let you take full advantage of the amount of beans you get for the effort you put in. All types of beans, from green bean to chickpeas, are a safe complement to any diet. Rich in protein, the bean is one of the main components of a vegetarian diet, as well as a perfect side dish for those with a meat liking.

To those who work a greenhouse, the seed is the first stage of growth of bean plants. The plant-taking root has a much greater chance of high-quality seeds, which will result in a higher yield in your greenhouse. Although these seeds may be much more costly, the increase in the growth of bean plants is worth the investment, particularly if you wish to have a wider garden.

If the temperature drops no less than 61 degrees F or 16 degrees C, planting should be performed to optimize the growth of the bean plants. When the temperature drops below this point, it will not take root from your plants and will die.

After the seeds have been planted, the time it takes for the plant to enter the seedling stage varies from three to around 40 days, with an average of 11 days. A seedling is a very young plant that has just started breaking down the soil sheet. This step of the growth cycle of the bean plant is critical because a healthy seedling can develop into a more robust plant. If your seedlings are overwatered or dehydrated, your crops will fail, and the amount of beans collected later in the process will be lower.

It takes an average of at least 50 days for your plant to grow pods and be ready for harvest, from the stage that your plant has become a seedling. This means that these beans are likely to only have one growing period in a season. The sowing of beans will take place no earlier than March to ensure that your plants have had adequate time to mature before fall frosts hit during the season. Frost can cause significant harm to the growth of bean plants and caution should be taken to prevent this. It can be difficult in colder climates, as the time needed for growing bean plants is closely tied to when frosts end and begin.

The bean plant is an annual plant, meaning it can grow again for at least three growing seasons. Most gardeners would start from scratch, however, losing the old bean crop, and with each growing season starting fresh.

Bean problems

Like most plants in your garden, beans have a couple of enemies you must protect against. Several of the most common pests and diseases, how to recognize them and what to do about them are as follows:

Aternaria leaf spot – (brown spots on leaves) Ensure that beans are planted in fertile soil.

Anthracnose – (small, dark stem lesions) Make sure you water plants at the base and never on the stems. Often, crops rotate.

Aphids – (small soft insects that can typically be found on the underside of the leaves). If just a few leaves have aphids, just pinch those leaves off. When there are enough, soapy water works also planting companion plants that attract natural predators.

Blackroot rot – (long purple lesions on root tissue that can eventually cause plant death) Swap bean crops with non-susceptible grasses.

Cutworms – (these extreme or "cut" seedlings on the soil line) Ensure the removal of plant debris from the soil.

Loopers – (These insects can eat holes in the leaves and can be very destructive). To extract, handpick.

White mold – (fuzzy white mold on plant flowers) Ensure plenty of row space and rotate seasonal crops.

Beans make the best addition to any garden and there's something great for every garden, with so many varieties available. So, plant some old favors, or try something new!

How to cultivate herbs and their uses are traced back to ancient China and ancient Egypt. Only medieval papers and the Bible offer references to herbs most people use. The herbs can be used by gardeners in many ways when they cultivate them. Herbs are useful as food flavors, drying for potpourri, teas, herbal remedies, and even keeping pests in a garden under control. A herb garden is mostly based on one particular function or another, but it does not have to be because in all these areas a combination of herbs can be cultivated for use. In a garden area, or indoors in containers, a herb garden can be grown outside.

Herbs can be cultivated in various ways from an indoor herb garden in a kitchen area to outdoor a small garden plot. Only an area of 4 feet by 6 feet will grow enough herbs for a family of small size. Although the primary purpose for these herbs is to use with food, others are grown solely for their aromatic foliage, and others are grown for the beautiful flowers, whether fresh or dried. Although several herbs are put on garnish plates or in salads, others are cooked to add flavor to the food.

As with all plants, herbs may be perennials, annuals, trees, or shrubs. You need soil that will drain well into which to plant your herbs. If your soil is dry, or too thick, it will help to add organic matter. There is no need to use fertilizers. Some herbs grow best in full to part light, but some do really like full shade. Most herbal varieties excel in afternoon shade. Surprisingly, the plants are only targeted by a few insects and diseases. The red spider mites may invade plants that grow low to the ground at times when the weather is hot and dry, and the aphids may seek out the caraway, dill, fennel, or anise. Rust will affect mint.

Herbal seedlings can be purchased in the garden setting of choice for planting, or herbs can be planted as rising seeds too. Nevertheless, it is a thrill seeing plants grow from seeds. This way, from sprouting to maturity and beyond, you can appreciate the entire growth cycle. By growing herbs, a gardener gets more praised because they're used for so many purposes. Virtually all the herbs can start from seed. Seeds need to be planted in a box or pot at the end of winter which is shallow. Using a light soil and drain well for planting the seeds in. Since herbs have a shallow root base, a limited amount of soil will be given to the seed upon a need to be covered. They shouldn't be sown too deeply. Follow this guide: the smaller the seed, the higher it should be sown. The seedlings will then be transplanted outdoors when spring arrives. Although most and not all of the herbs can be sprouted from seed, they do well to be transplanted. Herbs such as fennel, dill, coriander, and anise either need to be planted straight into the field or use peat pots to grow the seeds in. When the seedlings sprout, the peat pots can be planted straight down to the ground.

Even though it is worthwhile and simple to grow herbs in your home garden, you do need to understand and learn some knowledge about them. Much of the detail was stated in this chapter. Nonetheless, you need to read more about herbs, to find out more.

PROBLEMS GROWING HERBS

Herbs tend to be fairly easy to grow as long as you pay attention to certain golden laws. Many herbs love the sun and need at least six hours a day of sunlight. Herbs prefer well-drained soil with a pH of 6 to 7, and with some healthy organic compost adjusted. Daily pruning and, as a result, eliminating any low or infested growth are the final components for defending herbs against pests and diseases. That said, the herb garden can be plagued by certain may pests and herbal diseases.

Protecting herbs from pests A natural repellent to many insects is the essential fragrant oils of most herbs. Notwithstanding this, pests like slugs intrude the herb garden at some point and ravage your plants. However, lots of these pests are not significantly harmful, and are just a nuisance.

Aphids – Aphids love the tender new herb leaves and can induce curling of the leaves in large numbers. The resulting secretion of honeydew can both encourage sooty mold and attract ants. Aphids are found most frequently among crowded and fast-growing herbs. Horticultural soaps and neem oil can help to exterminate these plagues.

Spider mites – Spider mites prefer soft, dry conditions and are frequently seen on herb leaves' undersides. Protecting the herb garden from these pests is as easy as a good stream of water directed at the foliage and daily watering.

Herbal Diseases

Very few herbs (mints and lemongrass) survive in humid soil. Waterlogged soils foster fungal diseases such as root rot in fusariums. Symptoms occur as brown lines on herb stems with an end result sometimes arising from the plant's general collapse. Rust plagues several members of the mint family and occurs on the underside of the leaves as rusty orange lesions. Proper growing conditions, irrigation, elimination of damaged or otherwise infested foliage and daily pruning are protections against herbal diseases. Raised beds should encourage good morning drainage and watering to allow the herb plenty of time to dry out will also slow the spread of fungal spores that could lead to disease.

Troubleshooting the Herb Garden

As they suggest, the best defense is a strong offense, so remember to obey the golden rules as illustrated below when troubleshooting the herb garden: select safe herbs to be planted. In the right climate, plant the safe herb either moist and humid, or sunny and dry. Do your research and find the best place for growing herb type. Do not overpopulate your herbal plants. Enable growth, propagation, and general aeration between plants. Practice good rinsing and fertilizing. Irrigate and fertilize (preferably with organic food such as compost tea) on a schedule and allow the water to dry between. Weed between plants also helps to deter pests and encourage safe foliage and root systems. Prune, prune, prune...Prune. Prune your weed, or to put it another way, always harvest the weed plant. Not only will this immediately prompt you to remove any sick vegetation and detect any marauding insects for removal, but it will also encourage a lusher, bushier specimen. Harvesting will also remove blossoms, which will keep the plant growing as flowering is a warning to the plant that it is about time for the season to die back.

Problems When Growing Herbs

Fortunately, herbs typically do not suffer from problems that other plants may have. Problems such as insect pests and diseases are uncommon, so shortages in nutrients are impossible. Too much or inadequate watering can be a problem, but this can typically be easily rectified. Another issue is that certain herbs grow quickly. Plants such as the mint and lemon balm can quickly take over the plot and swamp other plants' production.

Although they're rare, issues do occur from time to time, so it's important to know what to do if your herbs get into trouble.

Aphids and Other Insect Pests

Aphids are drawn to luscious leafy growth and can damage herbs like basil and cilantro. Greenfly or blackfly are the most common aphids. They come together at the top of the plants and surround new growth areas. Sucking the sap from the plants, they secrete a sticky sweet solution. Ants love to drink this remedy, and you sometimes see them on plants "farming" aphids and collecting the delicious secretions.

As aphids are drawn to the lush, new plant growth, they are more likely to target plants fed with artificial fertilizers. Artificial fertilizers induce lush new growth and also weaken the ability of plants to fend off pest attacks. What's more, artificial fertilizer-fed herbs don't taste as well as natural herbs. Since the soil is fertile and provides an abundance of organic matter, extra nutrients need not be supplied.

If aphids invade your plants, rubbing them off with your fingertips or spraying the infestation with a stream from your hose is the best way to kill them. Also, you could grow flowers like candytuft and marigolds to attract ladybirds and lacewings to the area. They'll feast happily on the aphids that trouble your herbs. Do not use pesticides. They are harmful to the plant.

HERBS AND DISEASE

Disease in herbs is seasonal, but it may occur during a dry, wet summer particularly.

Herbs can be a problem with the following diseases:

eases:

Chives – downy mildew and rust.

Dill – rusty heart, phoma blight, and stem rot.

French tarragon – thick and wet soil root rot.

Basil and Oregano – powdery mildew-root rot.

Growing Problems

When put in a sunny position in fertile, free-draining soil most herbs get on very happily. Often, though, they'll grow too much or not grow enough.

Herbs capable of becoming overgrown are mint and lemon balm. They will take over the plot and stop other herbs growing in the plot. Grow them in pots to prevent this, then drop the pots into the soil. This will restrict their root growth and prevent them from spreading where they aren't needed.

Certain issues affecting herbal growth include are inadequate light – most herbs require plenty of sunlight to thrive. Seek to switch your herbs to places where they can get more sunlight.

Waterlogging – if you have heavy clay soil water you may have difficulty draining away, particularly if it has been raining for an extended period of time. When adding plenty of organic matter, such as compost or well-rotted manure and grit, break up the soil. Instead, the herbs in a pot grow in a soil-based compost.

Nutrient deficiency – if the leaves of your herbs look yellow or brown at the ends and the soil is not too dry or too wet, or the soil may not have enough nutrients. Apply an organic liquid feed to raise the plant, then bring in the autumn organic matter for instance, compost or well-rotted animal manure to provide nutrients for next season.

Seed running – annual herbs like coriander and basil can be a probe to run to seed in hot weather. This means that they start flower production early, rather than producing lots of luscious leaves, and produce seeds which slow or stop new leaves from growing. Different factors may contribute to this, including stress. High temperatures are the most common. To avoid this from happening cultivate the plants in slightly shady areas.

Your herbs would not experience any issues. It's crucial not to be panic when they do, though. Predators such as ladybirds and lacewings can eat bugs, and annual herbs can be re-seeded – they'll be ready in a few weeks.

PROPAGATION REQUIREMENTS OF POTATOES

Potatoes are cool seasonal crops that best grow in cooler climates, or as a winter crop in warm summer areas. They're heat prone but can withstand a light frost. Potatoes require a rich, moist, loose, well-draining soil with a pH of between 5.8 and 6.5 and will develop optimally at daytime temperatures between 18 and 27 ° C (65–80 ° F) and 12 to 18 ° C (55–65 ° F) at nighttime temperatures. Plants can also be successfully grown in burlap bags or in large containers outdoors. Potato seed parts are typically grown from seed potatoes. It is possible to use small portions of a large tuber known as seed bits, or small seed potatoes. When in season and through seed firms, seed potatoes can be bought from garden centers. Growing piece of material that is planted should have at least two eyes. The eyes are the region from which a shoot can sprout and should be allowed to cure for a few days before it is planted in the soil after cutting. Curing helps prevent the seed fragments from rotting and also reduces the risk of contracting a pathogen. Curing is very easy and can be done by placing the seed pieces on paper towels and allowing for 3 to 4 days of drying out. Seed potatoes and parts could be planted from 0–2 weeks after the last frost, or immediately the soil is workable in early spring, keeping in mind that a freeze will kill the plants. Working in compost or well-rotted manure prepares the soil for planting. Potatoes are usually cultivated in hilled rows. This will include digging 60–90 cm (2–3 ft) apart shallow trenches after applying the compost or manure. Place the seed pieces apart by 30 cm (12 in) and cover with 7.5 cm (3 in) of soil. If the plants reach around 25 cm (10 in) in height, the soil piles up around the plant stems to cover them up to around half of their height. That prevents shallow tubers from turning green from sunlight exposure. Let the plants grow another 25 cm (10 in) and mound the soil again. Continue this cycle for crop growth length. Straw may be used around the plants instead of soil that reduces the importance to dig for the tubers, care must be taken to periodically add the straw fresh because it breaks down over time. Additionally, they may grow potatoes in containers or burlap bags. Potatoes are soil moisture sensitive and grow best when soil moisture is constant. The plants typically need around 1 inch of rainfall or irrigation water per week. Water-saturated soil should be avoided, as tubers and rot can form poorly.

Furthermore, potatoes are heavy feeders, and every two weeks the addition of a balanced fertilizer can help to increase tuber yields.

Harvesting

The time it takes for potato tubers to mature is variable and depends on the variety being grown, although it usually takes about 2-3 weeks after the plants have flowered. All tubers should be harvested on the death of the vines or before a frost that kills the plants. Harvest the tubers by digging them gently with a fork or hands if the soil is sufficiently loose. Harvesting is easier with dry soil. Before storage, do not wash the tubers.

PROPAGATION REQUIREMENTS OF MAIZE

Maize is best grown in dry, tropical and subtropical regions as it needs dry soils for optimal growth. A high-quality soil which is rich, fertile and well-draining with a pH between 6.0 and 6.8 is one of the most important requirements for growing maize. Maize plants are heavy feeders, and even the most fertile soils may need nutrient supplements as plants especially develop nitrogen. As it grows, maize also requires plenty of room and is pollinated by water. It should be planted where, for most of the day, it receives full sunlight and provides ample moisture.

Dates of maize planting rely on the variety being cultivated. Varieties should be sow when the soil has warmed up to a minimum of 12.7 ° C (55 ° F) and when the soil reaches 18.3 ° C (65 ° F). By spreading black plastic mulches about a week before planting, soil can be brought up to temperature faster. Sowing seeds should be approximately 2.5 cm (1 in.) deep and 10–15 cm (~3–4 in) apart, making 76–91 cm (~30–36 in) between rows. Maize also should be planted in blocks (numerous rows) rather than in a single long row, because it is pollinated by wind and pollen can pass much more easily between plants. Once the seedlings are around 7.5–10.0 cm (3–4 in) in height, they will be thinned to a final width of 20–30 cm (8–12 inches). Stagger maize plantings to ensure continuous harvest during the summer period.

GENERAL CARE AND MAINTENANCE

Maize plants are heavy feeders, especially nitrogen (N) and care should be taken in applying fertilizer to provide them with adequate nutrients. Upon planting, maize undergoes a rapid growth cycle of between 30 and 40 days and should be fertilized just before that. To ensure the plant maximizes the use of nitrogen, all fertilizer applications should be made before the tasseling time. Be mindful of the nutrient deficiency signs and plants will have a dark green color. Purple tinged leaves suggest a lack of phosphorus to the plants, while light green leaves suggest a lack of nitrogen to them.

Using fertilizer

Plants also require sufficient soil moisture to tassel and form silks during the growing season. In small to medium size plantations, soaker hoses can be used to great effect. Pollination happens as the wind conveys pollen from the male tassel to the female silk – silk produced a single kernel of corn, and partially filled ears are usually a result of poor pollination.

Harvesting

Each stalk of maize would yield one broad corn ear. The stalk will develop a second, slightly smaller ear under ideal conditions that reach maturity a little later than the first. Maize should be harvested at the "milk point" of growth when the kernels within the husk are well packed and when the kernel is punctured, they contain a milky material. Test ears to maturity by gently peeling a small portion of the husk back. Be sure to check the ears for maturity and harvest regularly as needed, as ears may easily become over-ripened and lose their sweetness. Remove the ears from the stalk by quickly pulling down while twisting, and then refrigerate until eaten.

Physiological Diseases

Nitrogen deficiency – The plant turns light green, a common symptom of nitrogen deficiency; a 'V' shaped yellow coloration on the leaves. This pattern begins from the end of a leaf to the collar of a leaf. The symptom starts from the lower to the upper leaves.

The deficient plants are dark green, and the lower leaves exhibit reddish-purple discoloration.

Potassium deficiency – The margins of the leaves turn yellow and brown, which show as firing or drying. Symptoms are moving from the lower to the upper branches.

Symptom of sulfur deficiency occurs on younger leaves where we see striping of yellow color (interveinal chlorosis).

Zinc deficiency – Upper leaves show large yellow bands and turn light brown or gray necrosis (dead-spots) later. The sign appears first in the center of the leaves and is spreading outward.

CONCLUSION

One of the most amazing reasons to keep your garden at home is that it's absolutely self-renewal. After you've bought seeds after, there's no need to spend money on seeds ever again. Everything you have to do is extract seeds from some of your harvested trees, fruits and vegetables and plant these same seeds the following year. Here's your guide to harvesting and storing seeds from your garden for next year's planting:

Begin with quality seeds. Yes, it's true that once you've planted a garden, you'll never have to buy seeds again. You do need to start somewhere, though, right? It is important that you buy quality heirloom open-pollinated seeds when you buy seeds for the first time. The reason this is necessary is because most seeds you buy from a seed catalog or have been hybridized in your local garden shop. Hybrid seeds are popular because they were bred to possess certain attributes, such as resistance to frost in tomatoes. If you harvest seeds from hybrid tomatoes, however, then plant these seeds, you don't really know what you're going to be getting. Seeds harvested from hybrid tomatoes can produce tomatoes with properties from either parent plant. The second-year tomatoes are very unlikely to be the same as the first season. You can end up with an unwanted vine, or not even bearing fruit. For this purpose, if you wish to harvest seed from your garden, you must start with heirloom seeds. Fruit and vegetables from heirloom seeds are the only ones worth saving and planting since this is the only way you can end up with plants that are the same as the parent plant.

Harvest seeds from the healthiest plants – When picking fruits and vegetables from which to harvest your seeds, choose from the healthiest plants at all times. Select hardy, colorful, and vigorous plants.

Keep a close eye on your plants – When collecting seed from your greenhouse, timeliness is crucial, you should keep a close eye on your plants. Annuals with flowers are the easiest variety to collect seeds from as they flower and go to seed in just one year. Once the seed pods have turned brown and dried up on the vine, seeds are ready for selection. Many seedpods open up naturally when they are ready and disperse seed. You should tie a small bag of paper or fabric over the seed pods to protect them when they look like they're going to burst. With vegetables, harvesting seeds is best when the veggie is almost overripe just before it starts to rot, as this helps the seeds to mature fully. A tomato should be left on the vine for example until it is big, overripe and very soft. Eggplant should be left to ripen entirely and fall to the ground. Snatch up your veggies as soon as they reach this level, lest they meet the insects.

Separate the seeds from the flesh – It can be achieved very quickly with pod vegetables and flowers. Just open the warm, mature pod, and extract the seeds. Break the vegetable in half lengthwise with strong veggies such as eggplants, cucumbers and zucchini, and take the seeds out with your fingers. Gently mash the flesh with pulpy fruits such as tomatoes, to separate the pulp from the seeds.

Soak the seeds – You'll need to soak them in plain water for a full 48 hours after you harvest your seeds. Extract all the seeds that floated to the top of the water after 48 hours and discard them. When seeds float, this is symbolic of being dry and infertile. Just retain the seeds which have fallen to the bottom. Then drain the water and scatter the seeds over a sheet of paper towels so they can dry.

Remove moisture during storage – This is when there's one secret to saving your seeds for the next year. Your seeds have to be kept moisture-free. They become moldy and rot when exposed to moisture. Make sure they are fully dry before growing your seeds in storage. Instead, each seed type in a paper envelope labeled. You will note that seeds are typically stored in paper rather than plastic, as this allows airflow and hence keeps the seeds healthy and fertile. Place them in an airtight container, like Tupperware or pan, until your seeds are in paper envelopes. Don't forget to mark your containers clearly with the type of seeds that they hold and the date you stored them.

The next year, plant the seeds – The fertility of the seeds is highly dependent on how they are processed. It is best for your home-harvested seeds to store them for only one year; a maximum of two years. If you want to keep seeds in long-term storage, it is best to look for seeds that have been specially packaged for this purpose. For example, the Survival Seed Bank could have stored for 20 years, with no seed damage.